OSPREY AIRCRAFT OF THE

Balloon-Busting Aces
of World War 1

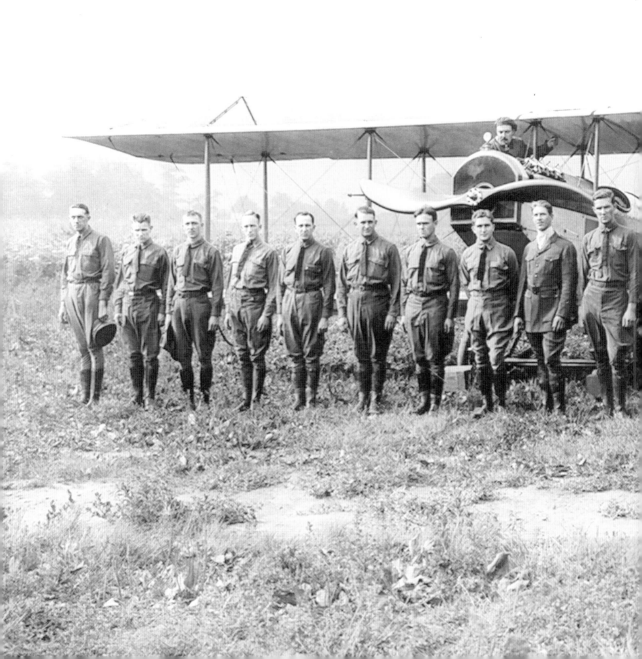

SERIES EDITOR: TONY HOLMES

OSPREY AIRCRAFT OF THE ACES • 66

Balloon-Busting Aces of World War 1

Jon Guttman

OSPREY
PUBLISHING

Front cover

At 0807 hrs on the morning of 15 May 1918, Adjutant Willy Coppens of the *9ème Escadrille, Aviation Militaire Belge*, attacked a German kite balloon over the Houthulst Forest, only to find the morning dew interfering with his efforts. After making three attacks through increasingly heavy anti-aircraft fire, he came in slowly at the *Drachen's* altitude and fired his last 30 rounds into it. Although he failed to set it alight, he did succeed in cutting its cables.

As he climbed over it, the balloon suddenly shot upward, colliding with his aeroplane. Coppens immediately turned off his engine, lest his propeller foul in the fabric, and waited in terrified suspense as his Hanriot HD 1 slid and tumbled along the sagging gasbag until it finally fell over the side. At that point Coppens dove earthward, switched on the engine and, when it restarted, pulled away while the perforated balloon descended to earth and exploded. It was Coppens' fourth confirmed victory, and he would score his fifth over Houthulst four days later.

HD 1 No 24 was destroyed in a German night bombing raid on the *9ème Escadrille's* aerodrome at Les Möeres on 13 June 1918, but Coppens would fly a series of others to become history's leading balloon ace – and Belgium's ace of aces – with 35 *Drachen* and two aeroplanes to his credit (*Cover artwork by Mark Postlethwaite*)

Dedication

This book is dedicated to all of those who braved the hostile skies in that pioneer era of aerial combat, and to all of those who strive to preserve their machines and their stories for future generations.

First published in Great Britain in 2005 by Osprey Publishing
Midland House, West Way, Botley, Oxford, OX2 0PH
443 Park Avenue South, New York, NY 10016, USA

ISBN 1 84176 877 4

Page design by Tony Truscott
Cover Artwork by Mark Postlethwaite
Aircraft Profiles by Harry Dempsey
Index by Alan Thatcher
Origination by PPS Grasmere Ltd, Leeds, UK
Printed in China through Bookbuilders

05 06 07 08 09   10 9 8 7 6 5 4 3 2 1

ACKNOWLEDGEMENTS

Thanks to the following airmen – all now 'Gone West' – whose recollections helped add a human touch to this tale of war; Pierre Cardon, Pierre de Cazenove de Pradines, Willy Coppens, Baron d'Houthulst, Alois Heldmann, Max Holtzem, Donald R MacLaren, Sir Hugh W L Saunders and Robert Waddington. Thanks also to those colleagues whose invaluable assistance in the scavenger hunt for photographs made this illustrated tome possible; Frank W Bailey, Colin Huston, Norman L R Franks, Roberto Gentilli, Alex Imrie, Stuart Leslie, Walter A Musciano, Walter Pieters, Otis Reed, Alan Toelle, Johan Visser, Aaron Weaver and Greg VanWyngarden.

CONTENTS

A NOT-SO-EASY TARGET

Captive or kite balloons, also known as *Drachen* ('dragons', which was an Austrian analogy for Chinese kites) and 'sausages', represented the oldest form of man-made aerial reconnaissance. They had first been used by the Revolutionary French Army in 1795, but General Napoleon Bonaparte had abandoned them because he decided that the heavy, cumbersome equipment required to generate hydrogen for them slowed his armies down too much to make their intelligence-gathering capabilities worthwhile. However, more mobile observation balloons subsequently saw widespread use in European and American armies from the mid-19th century through the early 20th.

Even after the invention and refinement of the aeroplane, balloons continued to be a military asset throughout World War 1, since they could stay in the air longer, and more continuously, than aeroplanes, allowing an observer to scan a large portion of the front from a safe distance within his own lines.

The principal problem for early, spherical balloons was maintaining a stable platform in high winds, but at the turn of the century the Germans developed the Parseval-Siegsfeld *Drachen*, which was an elongated balloon with a large stabiliser underneath. Rudely nicknamed a '*Nülle*' ('testicle') by its users, the stabiliser worked in a light to moderate breeze, inflated by the wind itself and driving the nose of the gasbag up and into the wind without much deviation. Belgium adopted the design before 1914, and soon after war broke out other Allied and Central Powers countries also began using *Drachens*.

In 1915, Capitaine Albert Caquot of the French Army introduced a more streamlined gasbag with a large vertical rudder, but it offered little over the *Drachen* when

Weighted down with sandbags, a German *Drachen*-type *Fesselballon* sits in its 'nest' awaiting the next observation assignment during World War 1 (*Tom Darcey Collection via Greg VanWyngarden*)

This German *Drachen* type kite balloon is seen in Belgian use in Flanders in late 1914. At that time the British were still using spherical observation balloons, the Belgians being the first to adopt the more stable German design (*IWM Q55555*)

it came to preventing the balloon from pitching in the wind. In mid-1916, Caquot produced a newer design, with three air-filled stabilisers arranged around the body at 120-degree angles. This proved to be such an improvement that in 1917 the Germans began fielding a copy – the Type AE – and began phasing out their *Drachens*, although a few of the latter would still be in evidence right up until the end of the war.

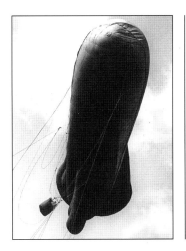

This Caquot type balloon caught in a heavy gale shows the improved stability that its three fins afforded compared to the *Drachen*'s single ventral stabiliser. In consequence, the Caquot design began eclipsing the earlier type in armies on both sides of the lines from 1916 onwards (*IWM Q27265*)

In contrast to the fantastic variety of aeroplanes developed during World War 1, virtually all of the gasbags were basically either of the *Drachen* or Caquot type. In spite of the predominance of Caquot-influenced Type AEs by 1918, Allied troops and airmen often continued to generically refer to all Central Powers kite balloons as *Drachen*, whether the sobriquet was technically accurate or not.

Communicating by telephone or wireless with forces on the ground, the balloon observers could detect frontline movements or direct any sort of artillery from a mortar attack on a precise target to massive, high-calibre howitzer barrages with murderous accuracy. As such, they

Two observers dangle from separate baskets beneath a Caquot balloon. The inverted cones beside the baskets hold parachutes in case the observers need to make a hasty exit (*IWM Q48044*)

constituted a very real menace to the other side's ground forces. Destroying enemy balloons, therefore, was a very desirable objective before a major offensive, defensive or logistical support operation was to be carried out.

On the face of it, a voluminous bag of hydrogen would seem an easy target for an enterprising fighter pilot, but for a number of reasons most airmen regarded balloon-bursting missions as extraordinarily difficult and dangerous. First and foremost, the gasbags were located deep within enemy lines, requiring their attackers to go after them while exposed to observation, aerial interception and every enemy soldier carrying a gun. Although the balloon floated several thousand feet above the ground, it could be rapidly pulled down by means of a powered winch when attacked, while the balloon company's attached batteries of anti-aircraft artillery and machine guns surrounded it with a descending cone of fire through which the attacking fighter had to dive.

Once he reached his downward-rushing quarry, the fighter pilot found it surprisingly difficult to ignite the pure hydrogen that gave the balloon its buoyancy, even with incendiary bullets. Only by pouring a sustained

Members of a German *Ballonzug* pose beneath their partially inflated Type AE balloon. While still generically referred to as a *Drachen*, the AE was in fact a copy of the French Caquot (*Greg VanWyngarden*)

burst into the gasbag, allowing some hydrogen to escape and mix with the oxygen, could the attacking fighter hope to touch off the fire that, once started, would quickly consume the entire balloon. If he failed to set it alight, the pilot had two options – give up and head for home, or gamble at even less favourable odds by making another firing pass through fully aroused, and consequently more intense, ground fire at an even lower altitude.

Once ignited, a burning balloon could be seen for miles, assuring confirmation for the fighter pilot who destroyed it, provided he returned to claim the kill. But the pyre was equally visible to the enemy, and the returning balloon buster faced a gauntlet of anti-aircraft and ground fire, as well as vengeful enemy fighters converging on his most likely escape route. Taken in sum, those factors caused attacking balloons to be widely regarded as a suicide mission, requiring as much luck as skill on the pilot's part.

Hydrogen bottles sit stacked and at the ready at a German *Ballonzug*. Even if they were not set afire, it cost time and money to repair, reinflate and re-raise damaged balloons. If an observer parachuted while under attack and the balloon was unharmed, it would have to be winched down and then sent up again (*Tom Darcey Collection via Greg VanWyngarden*)

Above
A German observer demonstrates
how to exit the basket if his *Drachen*
comes under attack. Early
parachutes were too bulky and
clumsy for practicable use in aircraft
until 1918, but they were standard
equipment for balloonists of both
sides (*Greg VanWyngarden*)

Right
An Allied observer's parachute
starts to open as he falls clear
of his balloon (*IWM Q48050*)

French soldiers adapt their versatile
75 mm field gun to anti-aircraft use
against a German bomber. Rings
of such guns surrounded balloon
nests, creating a cone of fire around
an endangered gasbag as it was
winched down (*Jon Guttman*)

French ace of aces René Fonck, who hated leaving anything to chance, did not include a single balloon among his 75 victories, stating in no uncertain terms that 'I do not thus like to combat the enemy, and I prefer to leave it to the specialists of such attacks'. The few airmen who made a practice of volunteering for anti-*Drachen* missions were regarded as something of a special breed, possessed of a combination of pyromania and latent death wish known as 'balloon fever'.

Almost as rare as the balloon specialists were aircraft fast and sturdy enough to improve the odds of carrying out the mission and returning to boast of it. Among those considered robust enough for the task were the British SE 5a, the French SPAD VII and XIII and German Pfalz D III and Fokker D VII. By 1917 the most common means of burning their lighter-than-air targets was a mix of flat-nosed Buckingham bullets to tear the balloon and incendiary rounds to ignite the escaping hydrogen as it mixed with the air. Most were 0.303-inch or 7.92mm rounds, although in 1918 an 11 mm Vickers machine gun saw use with those balloon specialists who could get their hands on one, such as Willy Coppens.

In mid-1916, French fighters were also equipped with a set of air-to-air rockets, also called rocket torpedoes, developed by naval Capitaine Yves Le Prieur. Fired from six to eight tubes mounted on the interplane struts, with aluminium sheathing over the fabric panels that might otherwise be vulnerable to their backblast, the rockets made a spectacular show, but they were wildly inaccurate and seldom effective even at close range.

9

French ace Pierre de Cazenove de Pradines of *escadrille* SPA81 described his experience with the 'torpedoes' on 19 August 1917;

'One day SPA81's commander, Capitaine Raymond Bailly, asked for one pilot to volunteer to destroy a balloon at Montfaucon – I proposed, and trained myself. Arming my SPAD with Le Prieur rockets mounted on the wing struts – an electric charge touched them off – I soon found my quarry and dived fast as the machine gun batteries opened up. At the right moment I pulled up, the rockets fired and went in all directions in an impressive smoky display. When it cleared, I found myself flying at an intact balloon. The rockets had gone in every direction except at the target! I withdrew, with only one bullet through my aeroplane. The next day I returned with phosphorus bullets in my machine gun and flamed that balloon.'

It was Cazenove's only balloon victory out of a wartime total of seven.

SQUADRON BUSINESS

This aerial view of a typical Caquot in operation shows the vast panoramic view available to its observer – and precisely why its elimination by the other side was frequently a strategic necessity (*Jon Guttman*)

lthough a lone eccentric braving the odds in his obsession to score a spectacular – and easily confirmed – kill is a popular image of the World War 1 balloon buster, a good many such aces accumulated their scores in the process of carrying out assigned missions, often in flight or even squadron strength. There were times, after all, when the elimination of even an entire line-up of kite balloons was

Nieuport 16 N976 of *Escadrille* N95, *Camp Retranché de Paris*, in which Adjutant Joseph Henri Guiguet test-fired Capitaine de Vaisseau Yves Le Prieur's 'rocket torpedoes', seen here attached to the interplane struts, in April 1916 (*SHAA B92.3135*)

desirable in preparation for a coming offensive so as to improve the chances that a local build-up of troops and firepower might go unobserved by the enemy.

The first operational use of Le Prieur anti-balloon rockets was a wholesale affair. In the spring of 1916, the command of the French *IIe Armée* in the Verdun sector, under Général Robert Nivelle, laid plans for a counterattack that would retake Fort Douaumont from the Germans. The assault was scheduled for 22 May, during which Capitaine Auguste le Révérend's *Groupe des Escadrilles de Chasse* was tasked with attacking any German reconnaissance aeroplane that ventured over or near the frontlines.

Meanwhile, Capitaine Le Prieur and Sgt Joseph Henri Guiguet (a pilot from *escadrille* N95 of the *Camp Retranché de Paris*, which had been testing Le Prieur's rockets) arrived at Lemmes aerodrome, some 18 kilometres southeast of Verdun. There, a call was issued for volunteers to eliminate eight German *Drachen* from the area north of the Meuse River. The eight pilots who came forth to carry out this unprecedented mission were Capitaine Louis Robert de Beauchamp and Lt de Boutiny of N23, Lt Jean Chaput of N31, Lt André Dubois de Gennes and Adjutant Barrault of N57, Sous-Lt Charles Nungesser and Adjutant Henri Réservat of N65 and Joseph Henri Guiguet of N95.

On 21 May Capitaine Philippe Féquant, escorted by two N65 Nieuports, reconnoitred the right bank of the Meuse to pinpoint the balloon nests in the area. Five Fokkers of *Feldflieger Abteilung* (Fl. Abt.) 62 attacked the trio and the formation's leader, Hptm Oswald Boelcke, sent one of the Nieuports crashing into French lines with its pilot, Sgt Georges Kirsch, wounded, for his second victory of the day, and his 18th overall. Notwithstanding that, Féquant brought back the necessary intelligence, and the following day eight fighters set out as planned.

Guiguet's target at Sivry-sur-Meuse, 30 kilometres northwest of Verdun, was arguably the most dangerous – its location on hills that gave the Germans an unobstructed view of the valley and both sides of the river made it of great strategic importance, and consequently its defences included Boelcke's fighter flight.

A clear, bright sky allowed Guiguet to quickly spot his quarry, and putting his aeroplane upwind of it, he dove until, judging the range to be right, he fired off all eight of his 'torpedoes' as the balloon was winched

Nieuport 16s, equipped with Le Prieur rockets and the pilots who volunteered to fly them, line up at Lemmes aerodrome before embarking on the weapons' first use – against eight targets at once – on 22 May 1916. Capitaine Le Prieur, in the dark uniform third from left, approaches the central group of pilots, which includes (from left to right) Louis Robert de Beauchamp, André Dubois de Gennes, Jules de Boutiny, Charles Nungesser, Henri Réservat, Jean Chaput, Barrault and Joseph Guiguet (*SHAA B77.767*)

Adjutant Guiguet of N95, Lt de Boutiny of N23 and Lt Dubois de Gennes of N57 await the start of their anti-balloon mission on 22 May 1916. A malfunctioning firing system compelled de Boutiny to return empty-handed (*SHAA B77.1546*)

Remarkably, six of the eight pilots involved in the 22 May mission destroyed their targets. The one sour note involved Adjutant Henri Réservat, who, after burning his *Drachen* north of Gincrey, fought his way through enemy aeroplanes, only to be brought down by ground fire. His Nieuport 16 (N959) was captured with half of its ordnance intact. The 'secret weapon' had not remained secret for long (*Jon Guttman*)

down to an altitude of 1000 metres. One missile chanced to strike home, and Guiguet's Nieuport 16 (N978) was violently thrown into a spin as the gasbag exploded into flames that he only narrowly avoided. Recovering, Guiguet made a beeline for Allied lines, pursued by several German fighters, but making it home unscathed. The *Drachen's* observer, Oblt Friedrich von Zanthier, was less fortunate, being killed in the attack.

Between Moirey and Grémilly, several of the other French *'torpilleurs'* enjoyed similar success. De Beauchamp destroyed his *Drachen* east of Flabas, but de Boutiny's firing system failed. Chaput and de Gennes burned their targets northwest and northeast of Ornes, respectively, and Nungesser, who had already scored his first balloon success over Septsarges on 2 April 1916, destroyed his target northwest of Gincrey for

his ninth confirmed victory. Réservat burned his *Drachen* just north of Gincrey, but Barrault's rockets missed.

As Nungesser and Réservat headed for home, they were intercepted by German fighters near Étain. Nungesser managed to scatter his assailants and fly back, but as Réservat resumed his homeward-bound flight, his Nieuport was hit by ground fire and he was forced to land, where he was taken prisoner and his aeroplane recovered with four rockets still intact. Le Prieur's 'secret weapon' had not remained so for long.

A few hours after the attack, the 36e, 54e, 74e and 129e *Régiments d'Infanterie* launched a full-scale assault on Fort Douaumont. Unfortunately for the French, an artillery barrage lasting several days, carried out prior to the actual attack to 'soften up' the objective, had already alerted the Germans to the prospect that something was in the offing. In consequence, they had already stiffened their defences and were able to halt the French just short of Douaumont.

Even so, the anti-balloon attack had achieved its objectives admirably, with six of its eight targets destroyed. The one sour note was the loss of Réservat, but he escaped from Germany on 19 March 1917 – to discover that Barrault had claimed *his* balloon victory. As a result of Réservat's testimony, Barrault was disgraced and transferred to the infantry.

Several French *escadrilles* came to specialise in balloon-busting over the next two years, and arguably the most active in that rôle was SPA154. The unit's top-scorer, Michel Joseph Callixte Marie Coiffard, was born in Nantes on 16 July 1892, had joined the Army on 16 November 1910 and campaigned against the Rifs in western Morocco a year later. Coiffard was a sergent by 29 August 1914, when he was assigned to the 13e *Bataillon de Chasseurs*. Badly wounded in January 1917 and declared unfit for the infantry, Coiffard took up pilot training and joined N154 on 28 June.

He opened his account with an Albatros two-seater on 5 September, and downed two more aircraft and was made a *Chevalier de la Légion d'Honneur* by 22 March 1918, when he was hospitalised. Upon returning, Coiffard found his unit being fully equipped with SPADs, and starting to take a serious toll on German *Drachen*. Coiffard burned his first in concert with MdL Paul Augustin

Sous-Lt Charles Nungesser of N65 faces the camera at left, with his Nieuport 16 N880 on the right. In spite of recent injuries, Nungesser, who had already burned a *Drachen* on 2 April 1916, was hardly one to turn down a novel mission such as the balloon shoot of 22 May (*Lafayette Foundation via Jon Guttman*)

A Nieuport 16 fires off its Le Prieur rockets. The prescribed method of attack was to dive at the target broadside at a 45-degree angle and loose the missiles at 120 metres. The more dangerous method of attack which saw the pilot close to within 100 metres of the target was still no guarantee that one of the *'torpilles'* would strike home (*SHAA B79.418*)

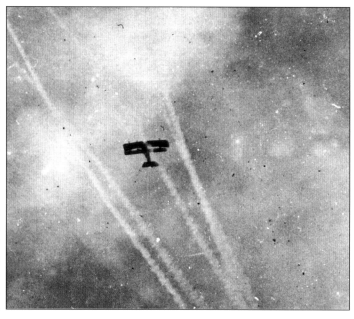

Lt Michel Coiffard, commander of SPA154, poses with his mechanics beside his Blériot-built SPAD XIII. Besides exhibiting the *escadrille's* red fuselage band, the fighter's wheels and cowl are also red, and Coiffard applied the name of his latest girlfriend, *MADO*, below the cockpit (*SHAA B91.5544*)

Adjutant Jacques Ehrlich and Lt Coiffard use models to give a graphic demonstration of how to dive on a *Drachen*. The two teamed up frequently on balloon-busting sorties in 1918 (*SHAA B91.5542*)

Edouard Barbreau and Jacques Ehrlich on 30 June, then teamed up with Sous-Lt Louis Prosper Gros and Adjutant Paul Armand Petit to destroy a second. All of Coiffard's partners that day would be listed among France's aces, although their status was based more on collective success and the *Aviation Militaire's* policy of counting shared victories as whole individual ones, rather than on individual exploits.

Whilst the SPAD XIII's high diving speed, sturdiness and twin machine guns made it one of the best-suited fighters for 'roasting sausages' during World War 1, SPA154's pilots had a penchant for tipping the odds further in their favour through teamwork, preventing enemy anti-aircraft fire from concentrating on any one aeroplane and multiplying the number of guns firing into the *Drachen*. Such tactics also improved everyone's prospects of survival during the frantic dash back to Allied lines should enemy fighters be encountered on the return route.

Coiffard's principal teammate, Jacques Louis Ehrlich, was born in Paris on 5 October 1893, and had enlisted in the infantry on 29 May 1913. However, inspired by the exploits of aces such as Georges Guynemer, he transferred to aviation. After a frustrating year in N154, Ehrlich finally scored his first victory with Coiffard and Barbreau on 30 June 1918. He joined Coiffard, Gros and Petit in burning a balloon over Courmont the next day, and on 5 July Coiffard, Ehrlich and Petit destroyed another between Courcelles and Sapincourt. Coiffard achieved a solo success over the Courcelles-Sapincourt balloon on 7 July, and on the 12th Ehrlich scored his only heavier-than-air victory when he, Coiffard and Sous-Lt Robert Waddington downed an Albatros D Va in the same area.

Born in Lyon on 28 October 1893, Robert Yvan Paul Waddington was descended from an English family that had established itself in France in 1800. The death of his elder brother, who was a Voisin pilot, led Robert to apply for flight training with the remark, 'Requests to replace his brother killed in aerial combat'. After scoring his first victory with N12 on 11 April 1917, Waddington transferred to SPA154 in early 1918. He resumed his scoring with a two-seater over the Somme on 12 April, followed by balloons on 2 and 9 June, before scoring his fifth victory with Coiffard and Ehrlich on 12 July.

Interviewed in Paris after the war, Waddington commented on SPA154, and some of its members:

'Coiffard was a real "trainer of men", a bit brutal, but of an exceptional energy and courage. Concerning Ehrlich, he was 100 per cent Jew as regards his aspect and demeanor, but quite non-religious, and nobody attached the smallest importance to the fact that he was "Israelite". I remember we had the most burning-hot quarrels about his cynical way of understanding life, but he was really very easy, and a good friend of mine.

'As you know, fighter pilots had long hours without flying during the bad seasons, and we practically never flew by night. So we used to play cards a lot, and Ehrlich was an ardent player of poker. SPA154 was well known for that. Was it due to the life of risks and perils we were leading? As fatality is concerned, we were more or less "fatalists" – death was with us every day, but "luck" was also a reality. Some of us had luck (my case!), others had not. Real fighters were doomed from the start if they had no luck. As a fact, we were all very young, and seldom mentioned death between us.

'I don't think there was any so-called rivalry between fighters and "aces". Each one did his utmost to help, defend or protect the others during a fight or an attack when flying in a team. Coiffard and Ehrlich are, in my opinion, a very good example in that matter: I am quite sure the idea of surpassing Coiffard never reached Ehrlich's mind. At least fifteen of their victories were achieved by both together.'

On 15 July 1918, Coiffard burned a balloon over Goussancourt in concert with his commander, Capitaine August Joseph Marie Lahoulle, Adjutant Claude Chevallier and an American volunteer from the Lafayette Flying Corps (LFC), Sgt Wainwright Abbott. A second fell to Coiffard, Lahoulle and Chevallier, while a third was despatched by Coiffard, Gros and Ehrlich. When the Germans tried to send up another *Drachen* at Goussancourt that evening, Lahoulle burned it at 1905 hrs for his tenth victory, but on the way back he was severely wounded in combat near Dormans – possibly by Uffz Reinhard Neumann of *Jagdstaffel* 36 – and just made it to French lines before crash-landing. Lahoulle was hospitalised and Coiffard assumed command.

On the 17th, Coiffard, Ehrlich and Sgt Louis Hubert destroyed two balloons near Moronvillers, while Waddington and Barbreau claimed another at Beine. Coiffard, Gros and Waddington shot down a Rumpler near Beine the next morning, and at 1915 hrs Barbreau and Abbott burned a balloon over the Forêt de Ris, while Coiffard and Ehrlich destroyed a second.

Adjutants Paul Augustin Edouard Barbreau and Jacques Ehrlich and American LFC volunteer Sgt Wainwright Abbott of SPA154 take a stroll between missions. All eight of Barbreau's victories were over balloons in collective efforts, including one shared with Coiffard and Ehrlich on 30 June 1918, one with Abbott on 18 July and two with Coiffard on 3 August (*Wainwright Abbott Album via Jon Guttman*)

The first day of August 1918 began with a triple balloon victory for Coiffard and Ehrlich north of Somme-Py, while a fourth fell to Waddington, Chevallier and Barbreau at 1750 hrs. Coiffard and Barbreau teamed up to burn two *Drachen* on the 3rd and Ehrlich scored a solo balloon victory on 10 August. During the next day's mission, Coiffard and Petit downed a Fokker D VII while en route to the target, which was burned by Coiffard and Ehrlich, after which Coiffard claimed another D VII on the return flight.

Lt Théophile Henri Condemine returns from a test hop in a SPAD XIII of SPA69. All nine of his victories were over balloons, and they were claimed between 22 August and 10 October 1918 while Condemine was serving in SPA154 (*Steve St Martin Collection via Jon Guttman*)

While flying in close formation shortly afterward, Ehrlich, blinded by sun glare on his goggles, ran his propeller into Waddington's SPAD. Both pilots managed to force-land unhurt, but Coiffard, recognising signs of combat fatigue in Ehrlich, ordered him to take a month's leave.

On 22 August, 23-year-old former hussar and infantryman Sous-Lt Théophile Henri Condemine joined SPA154, and while flying his first mission that same day, destroyed a balloon in concert with Waddington and Gros. Condemine downed another *Drachen* in a solo attack on 7 September 1918, and on the 14th he, Coiffard and Cpl Marcel Lisle burned two more at Gernicourt and Cormicy.

Lt Coiffard poses beside his last SPAD XIII, marked with the stylised crane adopted by SPA154 in September 1918, and bearing the name of his fiancée, *Valentine* (*SHAA B76.1198*)

Meanwhile, Ehrlich had returned, and on 15 September he joined Coiffard and Condemine in a lightning attack that claimed three *Drachen* in less than six minutes, as well as compelling the observer of a fourth to take to his parachute. In spite of their successes, the balloon-buster's Law of Averages began to catch up with SPA154 that day, as MdL Raymond Mercklen was killed by anti-aircraft fire and Coiffard had to

force-land his stricken SPAD near Trepail. Gros, at that point credited with nine victories, was shot in the thigh by a Fokker D VII flown by Ltn Oliver von Beaulieu-Marconnay of *Jasta* 19 over Bethancourt at 1635 hrs, and after struggling back over the lines, force-landed at Lhéry and was evacuated to hospital.

At 1806 hrs on 18 September, Ehrlich, Petit and Sgt Charles Peillard burned a balloon at Brimont after three low-level passes, but as they headed for home, they

were jumped by 11 Fokker D VIIs of *Jasta* 66. Peillard managed to escape, but Petit, victor over two German aircraft and four balloons, was shot down, soon followed by Ehrlich – either by the Fokkers or by ground fire while trying to evade them. Petit died of his wounds, while Ehrlich spent the rest of the war as a 'guest of the Kaiser'.

Coiffard burned a balloon southeast of Semide on 28 September and destroyed a two-seater southeast of Atienne on 2 October. Condemine's last two victories, on 3 and 10 October, were also the last balloons credited to SPA154.

After surviving so many anti-balloon missions, Coiffard's luck finally ran out during a melée with Fokker D VIIs over Château Porcien on 28 October. Although he scored his 33rd and 34th victories in the fight, a bullet struck him in the thigh and a second passed through his back, lungs and out his chest. Covered by Condemine, the iron-willed Coiffard flew 12 kilometres before landing near St Loup-en-Champagne. He was given a blood transfusion during the ambulance ride to Berenicourt, but it was not enough. Three hours later, Coiffard breathed his last. The following day he was made an *Officier de la Légion d'Honneur*.

Henri Condemine survived the war and went on to serve in World War 2, reaching the rank of lieutenant colonel. Jacques Ehrlich, who had been proposed for the *Légion d'Honneur* after his 'hat trick' of 15 September, but was not awarded it after being taken prisoner, received the *Croix de Guerre* with eight *palmes* and one *étoile de vermeil*, as well as the *Médaille Militaire*. He, too, served during World War 2 as a member of the French Resistance, and died in Paris on 10 August 1953.

The sort of team effort characterised by SPA154 was repeated in the quieter *VIIIe Armée* sector in Alsace-Lorraine by SPA90. There, Marseilles-born Sous-Lt Marius Jean-Paul Elzéard Ambrogi often flew SPADs alongside Maurice Bizot, Charles Jean Vincent Macé and Jean André Pezon to destroy most of the 11 balloons that were added to the previous three aircraft he had downed while flying Nieuport 17s.

Ambrogi was assisted by MdL Pezon in scoring his fourth victory – and his first balloon (a *Drachen* of *Ballonzug* (Bz) 143) – at Juville on 17 May 1918, as well as one from Bz 152 at Goin on 25 June. Adjutant Bizot helped Ambrogi destroy Bz 215's *Drachen* at Grande-en-Haye on 30 July, another of Bz 143's at Juville on 7 August and Bz 37's at Vaxy on the 21st.

Adjutant Paul Armand Petit of SPA154 sits in the cockpit of the SPAD XIII normally flown by Sgt Abbott and later by Sous-Lt Robert Paul Waddington. At least four of Petit's six accredited victories were over balloons prior to his death in SPAD XIII S15060 on 18 September 1918 in the same action in which Ehrlich was brought down and taken prisoner (*Jon Guttman*)

Shown beside his earlier Nieuport 17 decorated with the Sacré Coeur on the upper decking, Sous-Lt Marius Jean-Paul Elzéard Ambrogi was flying a SPAD when he burned his first *Drachen* on 17 May 1918. His last two, on 18 October, brought his total to 11 balloons and three aeroplanes destroyed (*Jon Guttman*)

Anti-balloon activity in SPA90's sector heated up on 2 September, when Adjutant Bizot and Sous-Lt Henri Dencausse burned Bz 62's *Drachen* at Geline, and Lt Ambrogi shared in the destruction of Bz 36's at Juvelize with Bizot and Pezon. Ambrogi and Macé were credited with a balloon at Bourdonnay on 15 September, while Pezon got another at Avricourt. The next day saw Bz 141's *Drachen* at Cirey fall in flames to Ambrogi, Pezon and Cpl Rivière, although the latter pilot was brought down by gunfire from *Flakzug* 98 and taken prisoner while trying to attack Bz 155's balloon at Saint Ludwig during the same mission.

Ambrogi's 12th victim, again from Bz 37 over Amelicourt on 10 October, was a solo success, but his last two on 18 October were collaborative efforts – one from Bz 211 at Omeney, shared with Macé, and the last, from Bz 217 burned over Avricourt, with Macé and Sgt Maurice Auzuret.

Pezon and Bizot were each credited with a total of 10 victories by the end of the war, while Macé had 12. The latter was killed in a flying accident at Haguenau, Alsace, on 7 June 1919, while Bizot suffered a similar fate on 27 November 1925. Ambrogi went on to fly Bloch MB 152s with *Groupe de Chasse* I/8 during World War 2, downing a Dornier Do 17 in 1940, and became president of France's veteran fliers' organisation, *Les Vieilles Tiges*, prior to his death on 25 April 1971. Pezon, who ultimately became a *Commandeur de la Légion d'Honneur*, died on 24 August 1980, aged 82.

Maurice Jean-Paul Boyau, who was another noted French balloon specialist, had enjoyed pre-war fame as captain of the French rugby team. Born in Mustapha, Algeria, on 8 May 1888, he began the war as a truck driver, but commenced flying training late in 1915 and after serving as an instructor at Buc, joined N77 in September 1916. This *escadrille* chanced to have so many athletes on its roster, such as Boyau and fellow rugby player Adjutant Strohl, and swimmer and sports magazine editor Henri-Joseph Decoin, that it came to be known as *'Les Sportifs'*.

Flying Nieuports, Sgt Boyau shot down an Aviatik on 15 March 1917, and his next success – a *Drachen* burned over Geline in concert with 19-year-old MdL Jean Marie Luc Gilbert Sardier on 3 June – was the first balloon and second victory overall for both future aces. Boyau burned another gasbag over Moussey two days later, and on the 24th he downed a scout, as well as roasting another 'sausage' in concert with Sous-Lt Marie-Auguste Joseph Charles Boudoux d'Hautefeuille and Sgt André Boillot between Nancy and Goin. Boyau and d'Hautefeuille downed an LVG on 13 July, and on 7 August Boyau made a successful lone attack on a *Drachen* between Juvelize and Bourdonnaye. Boyau and Sous-Lt Henri Rebourg destroyed another balloon between Cirey and Bois Bertram on 22 September, and a two-seater shared with d'Hautefeuille on 1 October brought Boyau's total for 1917 to ten.

Boyau's first balloon of 1918 fell near Beney on 3 January, and his second, on 20 February, was shared with Sous-Lt Sardier. The latter shared in the destruction of three Albatros scouts on 15 May 1918, and teamed up with Sgt François Guerrier to burn a balloon the next day. Guerrier, born in Treffieuz on 4 March 1896, had earned the *Croix de Guerre* with Bronze Star as an infantryman on 27 April 1917, before subsequently serving as a pilot in SOP234 and then moving on to N77.

Boyau burned a balloon over Bois de Bôle on 29 May, and on the way back he and Sardier downed an Albatros D Va. After claiming a Pfalz D IIIa on 1 June, Boyau joined Sardier in destroying two more *Drachen* on the 4th. Boyau burned a gasbag on 27 June, teamed up with Sous-Lt Claude Haegelen of SPA100 to eliminate another on 1 July, and on the 5th he again claimed a balloon and a fighter. Aircraft fell to Boyau's guns on 15, 17 and 21 July, followed by two balloons shared with Guerrier on the 22nd, and three more aeroplanes on 8 August.

Adjutant Guerrier joined MdL Joseph Thévenod, Cpl Maria and Brigadier Coquelin in destroying a *Drachen* on 3 September and went on to burn another alone, thereby achieving acedom exclusively on balloons. Boyau resumed his scoring on 14 September, when he joined Cpl Edward Corsi (an LFC member of SPA77) and Haegelen of SPA100 on a successful balloon strafing mission to Etraye. The following day Boyau teamed up with Lt Decoin, Sous-Lt Yves Barbaza and Adjutant-Chef Strohl to send two *Drachen* down in flames over La Haie des Allemands and Foulgrey, raising his tally to 14 aeroplanes and 20 balloons destroyed.

On 16 September, Boyau, Corsi, Cpl René Walk and Aspirant Henri Cessieux went after a *Drachen* of Bz 152 at Harville. Boyau and Cessieux destroyed the balloon, but then the French pilots were jumped by seven Fokker D VIIs of *Jasta* 15. Cesseiux and Corsi were wounded, but both escaped. Boyau evaded his first attacker and then, after diving under the burning balloon, tried to drive a Fokker off Walk's tail, only to be hit by either another German fighter, or by ground fire. Boyau was credited to Ltn Georg von Hantelman, but his flaming demise had not been entirely in vain – Walk, although credited to Vzfw Gustav Klaudet, actually survived his attack, only to succumb to Bz 155's anti-aircraft defences and force-landed short of Allied lines, whereupon he was taken prisoner.

'Les Sportifs' of SPA77 gather beside Sous-Lt Gilbert Sardier's SPAD XIII. They are, from left to right, MdL Jean de Laubier (missing in action on 3 July 1918), Sgt François Guerrier (five victories, all balloons), Sardier (14 victories), Sous-Lt Paul Maurice Boyau (35 victories, killed in action on 16 September 1918), Lt Henri Decoin (four victories), Sgt André Gelin (missing in action on 29 May 1918) and Cpl Richard Mevius (two victories, killed in action on 22 July 1918) (*SHAA B75.630*)

Sous-Lt Sardier poses beside his SPAD XIII, which appears to be marked with a yellow, red-highlighted, number '8' (*Jon Guttman*)

Pilots of SPA81 get together for a group photograph at Villeneuve des Vertus in January 1918. They are, from left to right, Sgt Maurice Rousselle, Cpl James Alexander Bayne, Sgts Chaigneau, Henri Peronneau and Paul Guérin, Lt Jacques Leps, Sous-Lt Marcel Dhôme, Adjutant Gaston Levecque, Sgt Paul Santelli, Adjutant Léon Blanc and Brigadier Pierre Cardon (*SHAA B82.103*)

Gilbert Sardier survived the war with 15 victories (five of which were over *Drachen*) and became an *Officer de la Légion d'Honneur*. He was also awarded the *Croix de Guerre* with nine *palmes*, one *étoile de vermeil* and one *étoile d'argent*, as well as the British Military Cross. Sardier later served as president of the *Association Nationale des As* before his death on 7 October 1976. Awarded the *Médaille Militaire* and the *Croix de Guerre* with three *palmes* and one *étoile de vermeil* for his five balloon victories, François Guerrier died on 28 June 1969.

Another ace who, like Guerrier, scored exclusively over balloons was Pierre Cardon of SPA81. The son of an industrialist from Armentières, Pierre Marie Joseph Cardon was studying engineering at the *Institute Catholique des Artes et Métiers* at Lille when war broke out in August 1914, at which point he and his younger brother, Michel, joined the *5e Régiment des Chasseur á Cheval*. They were soon off their horses and in the trenches, however, leading both to apply for flight training at Avord. After obtaining their flying brevets in Caudron G IIIs in April 1917, both became instructors, but after Michel Cardon was killed in a flying accident on 10 September, Pierre asked to return to the front, joining SPA81 at Beauzée-sur-Aire on 15 December.

Although his new unit was largely equipped with SPAD XIIIs, Sgt Cardon flew all his missions in an older SPAD VII. He was wounded on 5 April 1918, but on 15 May he came into his stride during an anti-balloon sweep. Cardon burned a *Drachen* in collaboration with his commander, Lt Jacques Leps, then teamed up to destroy another with MdL Louis Chaigneau, who also went on to eliminate a third gasbag alone. On 31 May Cardon, now promoted to maréchal-des-logis, teamed up with Sgt Maurice Rousselle to destroy a balloon, and on 3 June he, Adjutant Alphonse Malfanti and Sgt Paul Guérin burned another.

'Among the persons cited in collaboration, Chaigneau, Rousselle and myself possessed incendiary machine gun bullets specifically for the balloons', Cardon commented post-war, 'the other participants having only ordinary machine guns. I never took a bullet in my aeroplane in any

of my balloon attacks.' Cardon's final victory, scored northwest of Soissons on 6 June, was also the most memorable;

'We were all so intent on the *Drachen*, that it was only at the last moment I looked around and saw that Leps and Rousselle were converging on me! I took evasive measures with the result that we did not collide, but I went through the flames and smoke of the exploding balloon. I emerged with my carburetor full of gum and burnt rubber. The rubbery stuff choked the engine and I had to glide in. My aeroplane was in a pitiful state, but I managed to reach our side of the lines.'

Sgt Pierre Cardon and his mechanics pose with the greyhound emblem of SPA81 which adorned SPAD VII '8' in which Cardon scored all five of his balloon victories (*Pierre Cardon album via Jon Guttman*)

Among balloon aces, Claude Marcel Haegelen may stand as the ultimate team player. Only two of the dozen *Drachen* he burned were despatched solo, the rest involving not only squadronmates, but mix-and-match team-ups with other *escadrilles*. Born on 13 September 1896 in Belfort, Haegelen served in the infantry before becoming a pilot and flying reconnaissance missions with F8. Training in fighters, he resumed his combat career with N103 of the famed *Groupe de Combat* (GC) 12 *"Les Cigognes'* on 8 March 1917, and on 11 April he attacked his first *Drachen* at Chavaille, failing to set it alight but at least forcing the Germans to winch it down.

Sous-Lt Claude Marcel Haegelen of SPA100 survived the war with 22 victories, including 15 balloons. Most of the latter were scored in team efforts with squadronmates or pilots from neighbouring *escadrilles* (*SHAA B76.523*)

Sgt Haegelen scored his first confirmed success over a two-seater on 27 May, and the next day he and Sgt Félix Durand of N80 forced down another whose crew was taken prisoner. Haegelen was injured while landing his SPAD VII, however, and he was duly hospitalised until 21 September.

SPA 100's Lt Poulin, flanked by his mechanics, poses before his SPAD VII which was marked with the *escadrille*'s '*Hirondelle*' insignia. Poulin shared in the destruction of a *Drachen* with Haegelen at Hannonville at 1615 hrs on 17 September 1918. Cpl Maufras was brought down in French lines while returning from the mission and rejoined SPA100 the next day. Poulin also shared in the destruction of an enemy aeroplane with Maufras ten days later (*Jon Guttman*)

On February 7, he left the 'Storks', was commissioned a sous-lieutenant and on 11 March joined SPA100. There, Haegelen resumed his scoring in earnest, albeit usually in collaboration with other pilots from his own *escadrille*, such as MdL Pierre Schuster in his first confirmed balloon victory on 6 June 1918, or neighbouring ones as with his second, shared with Boyau of SPA77 on 1 July. By 5 November, when Haegelen transferred to SPA89, his total of 22 included 12 balloons destroyed, of which only two were solo efforts.

Chief test pilot for Hanriot after the war, and an active member of the French Resistance during World War 2, Haegelen was made a *Grand Officier de la Légion d'Honneur* before his death on 24 May 1950.

——— RFC, RNAS AND RAF SUCCESSES ———

In contrast to other combatant air arms, Britain's Royal Flying Corps (RFC), Royal Naval Air Service (RNAS) and Royal Air Force (RAF) approached 'balloon-busting' the way they did personal markings – they generally discouraged flamboyant individualism. Eliminating an offending kite balloon was just another squadron task to be done as the situation warranted, either by a volunteer or an assigned pilot. Most pilots considered it a dirty job, but when a gasbag was calling artillery fire on 'Tommies' in the trenches or spying on preparations for the next dash 'over the top', well somebody had to do it.

When it came to 'roasting sausages', the RAF's No 84 Sqn boasted more than one distinction. Its aeroplane, the SE 5a, was singularly well-suited to the mission, being fast – especially in a dive – and rugged for its day. Amongst the unit's ranks were included numerous skilled aces, many of whom had destroyed at least one *Drachen*. It also had no fewer than nine pilots of the US Army Air Service (USAS) on temporary assignment – more than any one British squadron in France – and the aggressive Americans were always keen to take on anything, including balloons. Among the unit's principal claims to fame, however, was the production of the RAF's leading balloon ace, Anthony Frederick Weatherby Beauchamp-Proctor.

Born on 4 September 1894 in Mossel Bay, Cape Province, South Africa, the second and youngest son of J J Proctor, Anthony adopted his mother's maiden name of Weatherby and added the 'Beauchamp' himself! Educated at George, Mafeking and the Old South African College, he later studied engineering at the University of Cape Town.

In 1915 Proctor served three months as a signaller in the Duke of Edinburgh's Own Rifles, during which time he took part in the campaign in German South West Africa. After returning to his engineering studies, in March 1917 he was persuaded by Maj A M Miller to enlist in the RFC as an air

No 84 Sqn's 'Procky' Proctor smiles from the cockpit of his SE 5a, assigned to 'C' Flight. Only 5 ft 2 in tall, South African Proctor needed extensions to reach the rudder pedals and another to pull down his overhead Lewis gun for reloading, but 'B' Flight commander, and fellow South African, Hugh W A 'Dingbat' Saunders claimed that his short stature and light weight enhanced his fighter's performance! (*Jon Guttman*)

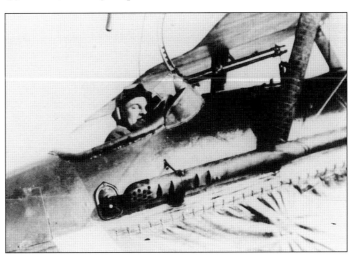

Capt Anthony Weatherby Beauchamp-Proctor (left) chats with Maj William Sholto-Douglas, CO of No 84 Sqn (*Steve St Martin Collection via Jon Guttman*)

Pilots of No 84 Sqn in early August 1918. They are, from left to right, Lt I C Simpson, Capts Sidney W Highwood and A W Beauchamp-Proctor and Lt Joseph E Boudwin, USAS (*Fleet Air Arm Museum JMB/GSL Collection*)

mechanic. Once in England he trained as a pilot, making his first flights in Maurice Farman Shorthorns in May. Proctor then joined No 84 Sqn under Maj William Sholto Douglas, which on 23 September 1917 was sent to Estrée Blanche aerodrome as part of the 9th Wing.

Assigned to 'B' Flight under Capt K M St C G Leask, Proctor gradually acquired experience until 22 November, when he gave Capt Edward R Pennell an uncredited assist in burning a balloon and driving another down. Right after that attack, Proctor lost his bearings and crashed at Belle Eglise!

As time went on he became increasingly aggressive, squadronmate Lt Robert E Duke stating that he would, and did, attack anything, oblivious to all dangers.

On New Year's Day 1918, No 84 Sqn moved to Flez, and on the 3rd Proctor sent a two-seater diving 'out of control' for his first confirmed victory. Following a fortnight's leave, the diminutive South African came into his own, downing nine more enemy aeroplanes between 15 February and 23 April. He more than doubled his score between 9 and 31 May, but it was not until 1 June that Proctor scored his first confirmed balloon kill southeast of Fricourt, harassing a second sufficiently to convince its observer to take to his parachute. On 5 June he teamed up with South African squadronmate Lt Walter Alfred Southey to send a Rumpler crashing west of Moreuil, and the following day Proctor burned two balloons northwest of Proyart and north of Bray.

On 7 June his CO, Maj Sholto Douglas, sent a recommendation to the commander of the 22nd (Army) Wing to award the Distinguished Service Order (DSO) to Proctor, noting that, 'He is a fine patrol leader and has on many occasions when leading large formations shown the greatest skill in aerial tactics. His keenness and courage are beyond praise'.

Two fighters fell to Proctor's guns on 11 June, and another balloon east of Contoire two days later. Heavy ground gun fire prevented Proctor from burning a second balloon, but not before he claimed to have seen its observer fall back into the basket after trying to bail out – likely hit by Proctor's gunfire.

On 6 August Proctor returned to No 84 Sqn from leave and a recruiting trip just in time to receive new SE 5a E5937, and to participate in the great British offensive east of Amiens two days later. Among the orders the 22nd Wing received on the 8th was a call for Nos 24 and 84 Sqns to detail one flight each to either burn or drive to ground all enemy balloons in the area. The first success for the latter unit came at 0945 hrs when a balloon was destroyed east of Harbonnières by Lt Norman W R Mawle. This was his fourth balloon and 12th wartime victory, although he was wounded in the wrist and stomach by ground fire during the attack. Despite his grievous wounds, Mawle managed to reach his aerodrome.

Groundcrewmen wheel SE 5a F5685 of No 84 Sqn's 'B' Flight off the field at Bertangles (*Steve St Martin Collection via Jon Guttman*)

Proctor spent his first patrol of the day strafing German troops who were holding up an advance by British tanks, but in a later patrol, flying with Sholto Douglas and American squadronmate 2Lt Joseph E Boudwin, he attacked two *Drachen* near Rosières, setting fire to one and consequently causing the horses to which it was attached to stampede. An intervening Fokker D VII was driven down out of control by 2Lt Sidney William Highwood, a 21-year-old No 84 Sqn member from Morden, Kent, who would soon become a balloon ace in his own right.

Over the next two weeks Proctor joined in strafing attacks against the buckling German ground forces, and added five more enemy aeroplanes to his score. On 22 August he was ordered to attack balloons along the front facing the British III Corps. Diving out of the sun, Proctor fired 200 rounds of mixed Vickers ammunition to burn one over Assenvillers and emptied half a drum of Lewis rounds into another at Hem, reporting the observer to have bailed out, but that the gasbag itself failed to catch fire. He then charged through the German balloon line, failing to destroy any, but compelling the observers of six to abandon their baskets and bail out.

Proctor returned to his aerodrome to replenish his ammunition, including a drum of Buckingham bullets, and as his patrol passed Hem once again, he noticed the balloon still there, so he attacked again and had the satisfaction of seeing it descend in flames.

On 23 August 1Lt George A Vaughn Jr – one of No 84 Sqn's USAS pilots, who was by then victor over five German aeroplanes – spotted a balloon over Ham, and encouraged by his squadronmates' recent successes, decided to have a go at it. 'I soon found out it was a lot tougher than it looked', he later recounted, 'because the ground defence was very thick and heavy. My Lewis gun was loaded with flatnosed Buckingham rounds, which tore large holes in the balloon when it hit.'

Closing to point-blank range, Vaughn succeeded in burning his target, and in a subsequent patrol he and Canadian Lt Carl F Falkenberg

These SE 5as show the white wheels and overpainted propeller hubs of No 84 Sqn's 'B' Flight. C6457 in the foreground was flown by 1Lt George A Vaughn Jr, who was the most successful of the nine Americans serving with the squadron, scoring three victories in July 1918. He was flying E4012 on 23 August when he burned a *Drachen* over Hem – and learned that balloon-busting was more difficult and dangerous than he thought (*H W L Saunders album via Jon Guttman*)

downed a Rumpler near Maricourt. Vaughn was awarded the British Distinguished Flying Cross (DFC) for his double victory that day, and he later transferred to command 'B' Flight of the 17th Aero Squadron, USAS, with whom he raised his total to 13.

After downing two Fokker D VIIs on 24 August and a third the next day, on 27 August Proctor was ordered to engage balloons facing the I Australian Corps. The *Drachen* were protected by eight fighters, but keeping his flight beneath the clouds until he saw an opportunity, Proctor suddenly led American 2Lts Joe Boudwin and I P Corse in a diving attack that burned a gasbag 2000 ft over Flaucourt, then outran the pursuing German fighters to regain Allied lines. An hour later, Proctor spotted a second balloon over Mont St Quentin, and after pretending to fly south to draw its Fokker protectors after him, he dived into a cloud and then changed course to attack the *Drachen*. Diving through intense ground fire, he closed to 100 yards to set the second balloon aflame. Proctor finished the month by sharing in the destruction of a D VII with Falkenberg on the 29th.

On 1 September the Australians occupied Péronne, and two days later a patrol led by Walter Southey downed a Rumpler, after which Southey destroyed his first balloon. He got another the next day, while a second fell victim to Sid Highwood and South African 2Lt Cecil R Thompson. Thompson and Highwood each got a balloon on the 5th, and the 7th saw four fall to Proctor, Highwood, Corse and 2Lt Francis R Christiani. Southey and Highwood burned a balloon each on 14 September, and two more fell victim to Proctor and Thompson the next day.

No 84 Sqn outdid itself on 24 September when it claimed no less than nine gasbags, including three by Highwood, two by Christiani and one each by Proctor, Falkenberg, Lt D C Rees and 2Lt William J Nel. Proctor burned a *Drachen* on the 27th, and on the 29th Highwood shared in two balloons with Rees and Lt E R Miller, while three others fell victim to Rees, Christiani and 2Lt James G Coots, and Falkenberg destroyed one of ten Fokker D VIIs that tried to interfere. However, during a second mission that day in support of advancing British troops, Christiani was killed by ground fire.

On 1 October St Quentin fell to the British, and two D VIIs were downed by Proctor. The next day 'Procky' added another *Drachen* to his score, and the 3rd saw him, Highwood and Coots down a total of four Fokker fighters. Proctor and 2Lt A E Hill burned a balloon on the 5th, and on the 8th No 84 Sqn moved up to the aerodrome at Bouvincourt. Later on the 8th, Proctor downed a Rumpler in flames east of Maretz. Shortly afterward, he was wounded in the forearm by ground fire, in spite of which he attacked a balloon he had spotted, albeit without success. Upon landing at Bouvincourt, he was sent to hospital – as it turned out, his war was over.

The last balloons credited to No 84 Sqn fell to Southey on 14 and 22 October, although he and other members would continue to bring down enemy aeroplanes until 10 November 1918. The Armistice was declared the next day.

No 84 Sqn had claimed a total of 129 German aeroplanes destroyed, 132 out of control and two brought down in Allied lines, as well as 50 balloons. Of the latter, 16 were credited to Beauchamp-Proctor, but that impressive tally paled somewhat amid an overall score of 54. For his activities on 28 and 29 August, 7 September and 1 and 2 October 1918, Proctor was awarded the Victoria Cross on 30 November. Highwood's 16 victories included nine *Drachen* and Southey's 20-victory total included five balloons, for which both aces were each awarded the DFC and Bar.

After being discharged from hospital in March 1919, Proctor participated in a Liberty Bond drive in the United States. Upon his return to England in July, he served at a floatplane station at Lee-on-Solent, the Cadet College at Cranwell and with No 24 Sqn. He was at Upavon on 21 June 1921, practising for the forthcoming Hendon Air Pageant, when he took off in a Sopwith Snipe that was not fitted with the wooden blocks that 'Proccy' normally attached to the rudder pedals so his short legs could reach them. In consequence to that oversight, Proctor was trying to roll off the top of a loop when he lost control and dived into the ground at Enford. It was a tragically avoidable end to a brilliant aviation career.

'Beauchamp-Proctor was the star of the squadron', remarked Sir Hugh W L 'Dingbat' Saunders, another South African of No 84 Sqn who himself accounted for 13 aeroplanes and two balloons, six decades later. 'Proctor was a small, wiry man, very courageous and a first class shot. His example had a great effect on the morale of the squadron. He had approximately fifty enemy aircraft to his credit, including many balloons. The latter were heavily defended by ground machine guns and always a daunting target! Proctor's death in a crash after the war was a sad loss to both the RAF and all his friends and comrades.'

The SE 5a was also the mount of the RAF's third-ranking balloon ace, Tom Falcon Hazell, a resident of County Galway, Ireland, who joined the Army when war broke out and transferred to the RFC in June 1916. Starting out in Nieuports with No 1 Sqn, Hazell was credited with 20 victories and had been awarded the MC by the time he was posted home to serve as an instructor in the autumn of 1917.

In June 1918 he returned to the front as No 24 Sqn's 'A' Flight commander, reopening his account with a Fokker D VII on 4 July, followed by a balloon over Ovillers on the 17th, two more south of Harbinnières and Proyart on the 22nd, and another over Harbinnières on the 26th. Hazell accounted for nine aeroplanes before collaborating with 2Lt John A Southey to destroy a balloon over Meharicourt at 1210 hrs on 21 August, then eliminating a second solo ten minutes later.

The following day, Hazell once again dove at a balloon over Meharicourt, but in spite of four of his men flying top cover, a solitary Fokker D VII went after him. Hazell, who had managed to set the balloon aflame, dove toward the winch crew, which scattered, and then bolted westward, with the Fokker still in vengeful pursuit. A wild chase ensued, with the SE 5a and D VII hopping and dodging about telegraph poles, trees and the

The wreckage of Capt Tom Falcon Hazell's SE 5a B8422. The fighter was photographed at No 24 Sqn's aerodrome at Bertangles soon after the ace returned from the 22 August 1918 sortie in which he burned a balloon and had been chased, and badly shot-up, by a Fokker D VII whose pilot, Oblt Ernst Udet of *Jasta* 4, was credited with it for his 60th victory. The aeroplane was in fact written off, but Hazell survived the war with 43 victories, of which ten were over balloons (*Mike O'Connor via Greg VanWyngarden*)

church steeple at Marécourt, until Hazell took the time to strafe some German infantry beside the road to Arras. At that point the Fokker closed to within ten metres of the RAF fighter and shot the SE 5a up so badly that the D VII's pilot, none other than Oblt Ernst Udet of *Jasta* 4, came away convinced that it had crashed, and he claimed it for his 60th victory. In fact, Hazell managed to limp back to Bertangles aerodrome, but the fuel tank, longerons and propeller of his SE 5a D8422 were shot to pieces and the aircraft depot to which it was sent wrote it off as irreparable.

In spite of that harrowing close call, Hazell destroyed *Drachen* over Bernes and Gouzeaucourt on 4 September in just a matter of five minutes, and after downing a Fokker D VII on the 8th, he flamed his last balloon at La Fére on 2 October. Two Fokkers bagged east of Beaurevoir on 4 October brought Hazell's total to 43, ten of which were balloons, before he was given command of Camel-equipped No 203 Sqn. Awarded the DSO and DFC and Bar for his service in 1918, Hazell died in 1946.

Superb though the SE 5a was for 'balloon jobs', a surprising number of British aces scored five or more balloon victories in slower, radial-engine machines. In fact, Britain's first balloon ace, Capt William Charles Campbell of No 1 Sqn, flew relatively flimsy Nieuport 17 and 23 sesquiplanes to score an extraordinary 23 victories, including five *Drachen*, in less than three months.

Born of a Scottish father and a French mother in 1889, this relatively elderly pilot joined the RFC in 1916 and No 1 Sqn on 1 May 1917. His final success was a 'double' on July 28, 1917, when he burned one gasbag between Westroosebeeke and Gheluvelt at 1350 hrs and the other southeast of Houthulst 20 minutes later. When he was posted home as an instructor in September, Campbell was awarded the DSO to add to his MC and Bar.

The Sopwith Camel, with its short fuselage and the vicious torque produced by its powerful radial engine, was a touchy mount to master, but those who succeeded took advantage of its superb manoeuvrability to make it one of the war's nimblest dogfighters. Such virtues availed a pilot little when dashing in after a balloon, but no less than seven 'Camel jockeys' became balloon aces – although at least four of them had other, greater claims to fame.

Nieuport 17 A6644 of the RFC's No 1 Sqn fell victim to flak when 2Lt T H Lines tried to attack a German balloon with Le Prieur rockets on 18 May 1917, only to end up a 'guest of the Kaiser'. Squadronmate Capt William C Campbell had better luck in Nieuport A6670 the very next day, however, 'roasting a sausage' at Ploegsteert at 0730 hrs for his second victory (*H Hugh Wynne via Jon Guttman*)

Capt William Charles Campbell claimed five *Drachen* in his final tally of 23 victories, making him Britain's first balloon ace (*Fleet Air Arm Museum JMB/GSL Collection*)

The most successful of the Camel balloon aces was Henry Winslow Woollett, the son of a doctor from Southwold, Suffolk. Studying medicine when war broke out, he joined the Lincolnshire Regiment and took part in the ill-fated Suvla Bay landings in the Dardanelles in 1915. Joining the RFC the following year, Woollett was assigned to No 24 Sqn and scored his first victory in a de Havilland DH 2 on 3 April 1917 – he managed to add four more to his tally flying DH 5s that summer.

Awarded the MC, Woollett served as an instructor until March 1918, when he returned to France as commander of 'C' Flight in No 43 Sqn. There, he raised eyebrows among the conservative RFC establishment by sporting a leopard-skin flying helmet and gauntlets, and installing a customised spinner decorated with the head of an American Indian on his airscrew. Still, he soon displayed undeniable mastery of the Camel, raising his tally to 13 by 25 March. He then opened his balloon account by burning two south of Arras on the 27th. Hoping to confuse German ground gunners during his anti-balloon forays, Woollett applied an experimental camouflage scheme of white blotches over his Camel (D6402), but his superiors quickly ordered him to remove it.

With or without such customising, Woollett's next performance was a 'hat trick' on 2 April, in which he destroyed a *Drachen* over Thiepval at 1240 hrs, a second north of Bray 15 minutes later and a third over Méricourt at 1355 hrs. Ten days later, he downed a two-seater and five Albatros D Vs in the La Gorgue area between 1039 and 1700 hrs, tying squadronmate Capt John Lightfoot Trollope's one-day record set on 24 March 1918.

Woollett then resumed his balloon scoring, with two north of the Scarpe River on 22 April and, after downing an Albatros D V at 1510 hrs on 9 May, burning a *Drachen* northeast of La Gorgue ten minutes later. Woollett was still flying D6402 on 15 July when he burned a balloon over Dormans, and on the 19th when he destroyed one east of Bézu and another southeast of Bonnes. A Fokker D VII on 9 August brought his total to 35, for which he recived the DSO and MC with Bar, as well as the French *Légion d'Honneur* and *Croix de Guerre*.

Henry Woollett, who died on 31 October 1969, was the RAF's second-ranking balloon buster, but his 11 successes weighted against 24 aeroplanes suggests that he was not exactly a 'specialist'. The same could be said of Capt Arthur Henry Cobby.

Born in Melbourne, Australia on 26 August 1894, Cobby had been a bank clerk before the war. Serving with the RFC's No 71 Sqn, which was later redesignated No 4 Sqn, Australian Flying Corps (AFC), Cobby downed five enemy aeroplanes between 21 March and 20 May, before burning his first balloon over Merville on 21 May. On 30 May he downed an Albatros D V over Estaires at 1650 hrs and a balloon in the same area seven minutes later. Cobby repeated this performance with a balloon and

A line-up of No 1 Sqn machines includes Nieuport 23 B3474 in the foreground, which was with the unit from 16 July to 6 November 1917. Campbell scored four of his balloon victories, as well as the destruction of two Albatros D Vs, in this aircraft between 21 and 31 July, before being wounded on the latter date (*Fleet Air Arm Museum JMB/GSL Collection*)

Capt Henry Woollett poses in his No 43 Sqn Camel D6402 in the summer of 1918. The ace marked the aircraft with a green dragon motif immediately below the cockpit, D6402 being used by Woollett to claim 23 of his 35 victories (a tally which included 11 balloons) (*Mike O'Connor*)

Capt Arthur H Cobby enjoyed great success flying Camels with No 4 Sqn, AFC, in 1918. Credited with 29 victories – five of which were over *Drachen* – he was the AFC's leading ace (*Fleet Air Arm Museum JMB/GSL Collection*)

Pilots of the RAF's No 3 Sqn. They are, from left to right, Lts J E Mutty, E T Mott and G R Riley. London-born 19-year-old George Raby Riley scored 13 victories with the Camel-equipped squadron, five of which were over balloons (*Fleet Air Arm Museum JMB/GSL Collection*)

an Albatros on 1 June, but his next balloon would not fall until 2 July – along with a Fokker Dr I. His fifth, and final, *Drachen* went up in flames between Estaires and La Bassée on 14 July.

Cobby's total score by 4 September 1918 had reached 29, making him the highest-scoring pilot in the AFC, as well as its only balloon ace. Australia's only other balloon ace was also the only one to serve with the RNAS. Initially a flying instructor at Cranwell, Flt Sub-Lt Richard Burnard Munday became a flight commander in 8 Naval Squadron in the summer of 1917. Uniquely specialising in attacking balloons by night, Munday got four of them after dark and one in its shed at Brebières at 2200 hrs on 29 September 1917. He was flying Camel B6378 when he bagged his fifth *Drachen* at the relatively early hour of 1900 hrs on 21 January 1918, and his final score came to nine. Awarded a DFC, Munday became a major when the RNAS and RFC were combined into the RAF.

Born in London on 23 February 1899, Lt George Raby Riley of Camel-equipped No 3 Sqn RFC began his scoring with an Albatros D V on 22 March 1918, and he followed this with an LVG two-seater on the 27th. Riley downed his first balloon near Mory on 8 April, but his next five successes were over enemy aeroplanes. Then, on 22 August he burned a *Drachen* over Thilloy, followed by two more solo and a third with 2Lt William Henry Maxted on 27 September. Riley drove a Fokker D VII down out of control the next day for his 13th credited victory, after which he was awarded the MC.

Yet another Camel ace for whom six balloons was the least of his achievements was Donald Roderick MacLaren, who was born in Ottawa on 28 May 1893, but whose family moved to Calgary seven years later. An expert marksman, MacLaren, like most Canadians in the western provinces, had little initial interest in the faraway war in Europe, but as British losses became critical, he felt duty bound to enlist in the RFC on 10 May 1917. When MacLaren was posted to No 46 Sqn at St Omer, in France, on 23 November, the most remarkable thing his squadron-mates noted about him was that he neither drank alcohol nor smoked.

MacLaren first experience of combat occurred at the end of January 1918, when he closed in on one of three German reconnaissance aeroplanes and fired – and both of

his guns jammed. The German observer gestured that his weapon was jammed, too, so the antagonists disengaged peaceably, but upon returning MacLaren vowed to personally inspect his guns and synchronising gear before every mission thereafter. In addition, he said, 'I perhaps did more flying on my own between patrols and carried less ammunition – not over 600 rounds – to reduce weight'.

MacLaren's first victory was a Hannover CL III, downed on 6 March 1918, followed by an Albatros D V four days later. The start of the last great German offensive of the war, on 21 March 1918, saw MacLaren join in the general RFC effort to stem the onslaught – and achieve acedom. After dropping four 25-lb Cooper bombs on a German long-range gun, he burned a balloon at Biache St Vaaste, then downed two LVG two-seaters. He was credited with two two-seaters on 22 March and three victories on the 23rd, before destroying another balloon on the 24th. A two-seater fell to MacLaren's guns on the 25th, as did a Junker sJ I on the 27th. On 2 April he joined his flight in downing another two-seater, then he and 2Lt John Henry Smith destroyed a *Drachen*.

Ten more enemy aeroplanes had been claimed by MacLaren by 20 May, when he burned two balloons south of Steenwerck. His sixth, and final, balloon kill came on 19 July, but that was out of a grand total of 54 scored by 9 October. The next day MacLaren, who had never been wounded in combat, broke his leg during a friendly wrestling match with a squadronmate and was posted to England on 6 November. On 6 February 1919, Maj MacLaren was awarded the DSO, and the French later gave him the *Croix de Guerre* and made him a *Compagnon de la Légion d'Honneur*.

After assisting in the formation of the Royal Canadian Air Force postwar, MacLaren chose to focus on civilian aviation endeavours. He never attended squadron reunions in England and avoided discussing his past with journalists, although he would answer questions from World War 1 aviation historians, provided it was to keep the record straight, rather than glorify him. The fact that few of his own countrymen remembered him as a war hero suited him fine, but when Don MacLaren died on 4 July 1989 aged 96, his record stands as the highest-scoring Camel ace of the war.

On the other side of the lines, circumstances also brought some German *Jagdstaffeln* to the fore when it came to eliminating Allied balloons. A case in point was *Jasta* 67, half of whose 34 victories were over balloons – and three of whose combat losses occurred during antiballoon sorties. Three of the four victories scored by Vzfw Thilo Boelcke (cousin of the 40-victory ace and pioneer of fighter doctrine Oswald Boelcke) were over balloons, but his last, a *'saussice'* of the 85e *Compagnie des Aerostiers* at Montzéville on 20 August 1918, cost him his life as his Albatros D Va

The highest-scoring Camel ace of them all, Canadian Capt Donald MacLaren scored all 54 of his victories with No 46 Sqn between 6 March and 9 October 1918. Six of these victories were over balloons (*Mike O'Connor*)

Vzfw Rieger of *Jasta* 17, nursing injuries after being shot down on 16 April 1917, poses alongside Vzfw Julius Buckler's Albatros D III D.2033/16 *Mops*. Buckler scored his first balloon victory over one from the French 36e *Compagnie* at Boise de Génicourt in this scout on 26 April 1917 (*Greg VanWyngarden*)

Ltn Julius Buckler of *Jasta* 17 poses before his new Albatros D V, with the black tail of one of the unit's Albatros D IIIs visible at left. Buckler's aeroplanes usually bore the legend *Mops* on the fuselage side, in this case on a light (blue?) band. After downing a balloon on 26 April 1917, Buckler did some serious 'sausage roasting' in Flanders in the autumn of 1917, destroying British kite balloons on 29 and 31 October, two on 18 November and another on 29 November. He claimed his last near Tricot on 3 May 1918. Made *Staffelführer* on 22 September, Buckler survived the war with 35 victories and the *Orden Pour le Mérite*. He died in Berlin on 26 May 1960, aged 66 (*Jon Guttman*)

(6591/17) fell victim to the unit's guns. Both of Ltn d R Hans Quartier's victories were over balloons, but soon after downing his second on 2 September 1918 he was brought down by anti-aircraft fire at Crécy-au-Mont and taken prisoner. More fortunate was Vzfw Richard Rübe, whose five victories included four balloons.

The most spectacular of *Jasta* 67's pilots – in more ways than one – was Uffz Hans-Heinrich Marwede, who was a product of the late-war expansion of German air units known as the *'Amerika Programm'*. He longed to add his name to the pantheon of *Kanonen* whose exploits he had followed while in school. His first success was over a de Havilland DH 4 on 1 August 1918, but over the next month-and-a-half Marwede was unable to add to his score, while noting the balloon successes racked up by his squadronmates.

His big break came on 14 September, when *Jasta* 67 launched an assault against the French balloon line between Clermont and Verdun. Ltn d R Christiansen was credited with a gasbag at 1630 hrs, but in fact his quarry, from the *57e Compagnie*, was not destroyed. At the same time Marwede attacked the *25e Compagnie's* balloon and succeeded in bringing it down in flames. That encouraged him to fly on through the

This Fokker D VII was allegedly one of six brought down by machine gunners attached to the 6th US Balloon Company in 1918. The unit's most dramatic 'catch' was Uffz Hans-Heinrich Marwede of *Jasta* 67, who was shot down just moments after he 'made ace' on 3 October 1918 at the expense of the company's gasbag (*Johan Visser*)

mounting ground fire to burn another from the 30*e Compagnie* at 1634 hrs, and a third, from the 31*e Compagnie*, four minutes later.

Marwede's next opportunity to add to his laurels did not come until 3 October. On that day Rübe roasted a '*saussice*' of the 51*e Compagnie* for his fifth victory, while Marwede went after a balloon that had just appeared over Montfaucon, two-and-a-half miles behind Allied lines.

At about 1130 hrs, observer 1Lt W J R Taylor of the 6th Balloon Company, American Expeditionary Forces, was telephoning his groundcrew that 2000 ft was high enough for the time being.

At that moment Marwede came in at the balloon's level, hoping to achieve surprise. The manoeuvring officer on the ground saw the Fokker D VII coming, however, and immediately got on the wire paralleling the winch cables and shouted a one-word message – 'Jump!' While the accompanying sergeant removed his headphones, 1Lt Taylor cursed as he cased his binoculars and gestured for the NCO to go first. A US Army Signal Corps officer on the scene photographed the event as the sergeant's parachute opened, followed seconds later by Taylor's.

Meanwhile, as the 6th Balloon Company was rapidly winching down the balloon, Marwede's Fokker dived after it at 200 mph through a storm of 75 mm bursts and machine gun bullets. A shellburst holed his wing, but Marwede kept firing at the gasbag, which was down to 500 ft when he passed it and zoomed up, his Fokker reeling from the concussion of another exploding shell. Marwede had just regained control when he perceived the light and heat of his target bursting into flame.

Just as he jubilantly turned back for home, however, another shell sent his D VII heeling over, and he suddenly felt dazed and sick while something warm ran down his face. Fighting his controls as the earth rushed up at him, Marwede managed to level off in time to make a somersaulting landing that left his aeroplane on its back just northeast of his burning victim. Moments later, Cpl Ray of the 6th Balloon Company and Capt Clarkson of the 30th Infantry Division were extricating him from the wreckage.

Dabbing the wound to his temple, Marwede was relieved to discover that the bullet had merely grazed his skull, but his fighting career was over, just as he had achieved acedom. 'I was a fool', he muttered in German. 'I should have let balloons alone. It is a sad speciality'.

Ray did not understand Marwede's words, but surmised their meaning from the expression on his face. 'If you're growling about picking the wrong balloon, Jerry, you got it right', he drawled 'You're the second one this company has knocked down this week, and that's one hundred per cent'. By war's end the 6th Balloon Company's gunners were credited with six German aircraft destroyed, which was an AEF record.

Declaring war on Germany on 6 April 1917, the United States was a late entry into the war, but the USAS had produced several balloon

A Caquot of the 44th Balloon Company, American Expeditionary Force (*IWM Q.88518*)

A disheartened Hans Marwede of *Jasta* 67 is led away for interrogation by US troops, his face bloodied from the bullet which grazed his cheek when his D VII was struck by a well-aimed burst of ground fire on 3 October 1918 (*Greg VanWyngarden*)

aces by the time it ended. The most famous, 2Lt Frank Luke, was largely responsible for the persistent image of the lone, eccentric balloon-buster. Most of his lesser colleagues, however, were simply doing their duty. The latter included Capt Edward Vernon Rickenbacker, commander of the 94th Aero Squadron and American ace of aces with 26 victories. Like Luke, Rickenbacker was awarded the Medal of Honor, albeit on 6 November 1930. Unlike Luke, he was alive to receive it, and he had earned it by plunging through a German formation to down an LVG and one of its Fokker D VII escorts on 25 September 1918.

The American offensive into the Argonne Forest required the elimination of German kite balloons from the start, and the 94th did its part as 1Lt Harvey Weir Cook burned one over Grand Ham at 1845 hrs on the opening day (26 September). Rickenbacker burned his first balloon at Sivry-sur-Meuse at 0500 hrs on 28 September, while Cook bagged a second at Clery-le-Petit at 0606 hrs. Another member of the 1st Pursuit Group, 1Lt Lansing Colton Holden from Brooklyn, New York, who had previously served in French *escadrille* N471 before joining the 95th Aero Squadron, 'roasted his first sausage' near Dun-sur-Meuse on the 29th. That same day the 27th Aero Squadron's lone champion of balloon busters, 2Lt Frank Luke, was killed in the process of destroying three (see chapter three).

Rickenbacker destroyed another *Drachen* on 1 October, Harvey Cook added one to his tally two days later and Rickenbacker destroyed his third gasbag on the 9th. On 10 October, Brig Gen William Mitchell despatched the 27th, 94th and 147th Aero Squadrons to eliminate two balloons at Dun-sur-Meuse and Aincreville. Rickenbacker selected 1Lts Reed Chambers and Hamilton Coolidge to attack the gasbags at 1550 hrs, while the rest of the group covered them.

The Germans were equally determined to defend their *Drachen*, however, and *Jagdgeschwader* I (the old 'Flying Circus' of the late *Rittmeister* Manfred Freiherr von Richthofen, now led by Oblt Hermann Göring) gave the Americans what Rickenbacker called 'a regular dogfight', in which he claimed two D VIIs, Chambers got another and a fourth was shared by Coolidge and 1Lt William W Palmer.

Nearby, 1Lt Kenneth L Porter of the 147th Aero Squadron claimed a Fokker and shared a second with 1Lt Oscar B Myers and 2Lt Wilbert W White. Another was credited to Capt James A Meissner and 2Lts George A Waters and Ralph A O'Neill, while a fourth fell to 2Lt William E Brotherton before he was shot down in flames. Rickenbacker saw a Fokker on the tail of another 147th member, at which point White turned and rammed the Fokker head-on.

Rickenbacker was belatedly going to Brotherton's aid when he spotted

American aces Douglas Campbell (six victories), Eddie Rickenbacker (26 victories), James A Meissner (eight victories) and Paul F Baer (nine victories) return home aboard SS *Adriatic* in February 1919. Rickenbacker's former 94th Squadronmate Meissner was commanding the 147th Aero Squadron at 1556 hrs on 28 October 1918 when he burned a *Drachen* at Bantheville for his seventh victory (*National Archives*)

1Lt Lansing C Holden (left) poses with fellow members of *Escadrille N471* beside his specially marked Nieuport 27 in July 1918. Later flying SPAD XIIIs with the 95th Aero Squadron, 'Denny' Holden was credited with seven victories, including five balloons (*Walter C Avery album via Jack R Eder*)

1Lt Edward Vernon Rickenbacker poses beside his famous SPAD XIII S4523 '1' of the 94th Aero Squadron. Five of Rickenbacker's 26 victories were over balloons (*Greg Van Wyngarden*)

his friend Jimmy Meissner, 'smiling and good-natured as ever, with two ugly brutes on his tail trying their best to execute him'. Joining the chase, Rickenbacker fired a long burst and wrote, 'The Hun fell off and dropped out of control, the other Fokker immediately pulling away and diving steeply for home, and safety'.

For all the claims made over them, the Germans recorded only one Fokker destroyed – that of Ltn d R Wilhelm Kohlbach of *Jasta 10*, who parachuted safely after colliding with White's SPAD, and was subsequently credited with it as his fifth victory. Rickenbacker claimed to have seen one of the Fokker pilots that he shot down take to his parachute, but evidently confused him with Kohlbach. *Jasta 10* also credited SPADs to Ltn Justus Grassmann and Ltn d R Alois Heldmann, their victims presumably being Brotherton and Meissner, although the latter made it home.

Ironically, Chambers and Coolidge never did get at the balloons that had been the whole mission's primary targets. At 1410 hrs, however, a SPAD XIII of the 22nd Aero Squadron flew five miles into German territory, fought its way past several enemy fighters and swooped in at an altitude of about ten metres to burn two *Drachen* at Bayonville and Buzancy in their nests. The pilot, 22-year-old 1Lt Remington DeB Vernam from New York, had previously served in SPA96, sharing in the destruction of a balloon on 12 August. His daring 10 October raid earned Vernam the DFC, and he would subsequently be credited with three German aeroplanes before being mortally wounded on 30 October.

Harvey Cook destroyed his fourth *Drachen* at 0555 hrs on 22 October, to which he would add an LVG on the 30th for his seventh victory overall. On the morning of the 23rd, 1Lts Edwin P Curtis and 'Denny' Holden of the 95th Aero Squadron attacked three German balloons that had been directing artillery fire on American troops from Montigny, only to encounter enemy fighters, one of which they shot down. Holden pressed on, and in spite of having to clear the jammed guns of his SPAD on three separate occasions, he still succeeded in burning a balloon at 0505 hrs, for which he was later cited for the DSC.

On 30 October Rickenbacker burned two balloons for his last victories, while Holden got another. The latter also destroyed a *Drachen* on 3 November, and the following day he dived after one that was being winched down through intense anti-aircraft fire until he set it ablaze, also damaging its nest and adjacent buildings. That action earned Holden his fifth balloon kill, his seventh victory overall and an oak leaf to his DSC.

While Eddie Rickenbacker went on to further exploits until his death on 27 July 1973, Holden and Cook were less fortunate. Holden was killed in a landing accident near Sparta, Tennessee, on 13 November 1938, while Cook, participating in his second world war at the age of 50, fatally crashed in a Curtiss P-40 in New Zealand on 25 March 1943.

THE LONE HUNTERS

During World War 1, airmen came to perceive a fine line between colleagues with the courageous sense of duty to volunteer – or simply accept the task – to eliminate an enemy balloon as necessity dictated, and icy blooded individuals who enjoyed such missions. For a variety of reasons – some stated, some inferred by their squadronmates – a handful of pilots became obsessed with the spectacle of burning hydrogen, which, if nothing else, was seen by everyone for miles around, almost always guaranteeing confirmation. Against that, the dangers of intense ground fire and racing home through a gauntlet of enemy fighters became of secondary importance.

Courage among fighting men involves overcoming fear, but the lone balloon specialists generally seemed to have no fear to overcome. Their squadronmates called this condition 'balloon fever', and regarded the compulsive balloon hunters with a mixture of awe and detachment, best expressed by 1Lt Kenneth L Porter, a six-victory ace of the American 1st Pursuit Group's 147th Aero Squadron, toward 2Lt Frank Luke, the balloon-busting champion from the neighbouring 27th Aero Squadron. 'We all thought he was screwy. We tolerated him, but we didn't want to be like him. Who wants to be nuts?'

One of the earliest balloon specialists was Marcel Robert Léopold Bloch, a French citizen born on 21 July 1890 in La Chaux de Fonds, Switzerland. Volunteering for military service on 7 September 1914, he went directly into aviation, receiving his military brevet on 12 October 1915. In spite of being injured on 7 November, Cpl Bloch was soon back in the air, and on 19 January 1916 he was assigned to *Escadrille* N3, where he was promoted to sergent on 11 April. After being reassigned to N62 on 25 May, Bloch found his niche when he began attacking German

Capitaine Jacques de Sieyes de Veynes, commander of N26, burned a *Drachen* on 3 July 1916, but his Nieuport 11 (N1135) was brought down minutes later and he was taken prisoner. On the same day, Sgt Marcel Bloch of N62 destroyed a second gasbag for his fourth of five balloon victories (*Jon Guttman*)

balloons, albeit unsuccessfully, on 26 and 29 June. When the Battle of the Somme began on 1 July, the French launched numerous attacks to take some pressure off their British allies, including strikes against the German balloon line, resulting in five *Drachen* falling in flames – two of which were credited to Bloch.

Two more French-launched anti-balloon sorties on 3 July resulted in Pyrrhic victories. Capitaine Jacques de Sieyes de Veynes, commander of N26, burned one *Drachen*, but he was brought down and taken prisoner. Bloch burned another north of Frise, but his subsequent citation for the *Médaille Militaire* described the price he paid. 'On 3 July, charged with destruction of a balloon, he accomplished his mission after receiving two severe wounds'.

Promoted to adjutant on 16 August, Bloch was assigned to the Technical Service after his release from hospital, but on 1 October he was back with N62, destroying a balloon near Longuavenes, and he burned a second east of Bapaume the next day. On 23 March 1917, Bloch was sent with a French mission to the Russian front, where he was injured in an accident on 8 May, returned to France on 2 December and was again hospitalised in January 1918. Bloch was made a *Chevalier de la Légion d'Honneur* on 10 July 1918, to which was added the *Croix de Guerre* with seven palms, and the Russian Orders of St Anne and St George. Although Bloch survived the war, he died in Czechoslovakia on 29 March 1938, reportedly as a cumulative result of his wartime wounds and injuries.

France's highest-scoring balloon-buster had had aspirations of being a Catholic missionary when war broke out. Born in Montauban on 25 May 1889, Léon Jean-Pierre Bourjade served in the artillery and in a trench mortar unit before transferring to aviation and joining N152 on 13 September 1917.

Although the unit's crocodile insignia appeared on at least one of his SPAD XIIIs, on 27 January 1918 Bourjade wrote in his diary of a more personal touch – a French tricolour pennant with the Sacré-Coeur on the middle white band, which flew from the headrest of his Nieuport. Bourjade claimed that he was motivated to volunteer for anti-balloon missions by the two years he'd spent cowering in the trenches under artillery fire directed by them, declaring that 'the day I could bring one down in flames, it could be more than just a victory – it could be a revenge'. After several attempts frustrated by jammed guns, on 27 March Bourjade dived on a balloon near Gebersweiler, and as he pulled up amid a fusillade of tracers and shells, he was gratified to see it catch fire. By 20 May 1918, Bourjade had burned three more balloons.

Taking a three-week gunnery course at Cazaux, he returned to his *escadrille* in June to find that it had been transferred from Alsace-Lorraine to the hotter Champagne front, and was re-equipped with SPAD XIIIs. Coming fully into his stride, Bourjade flamed a balloon near St Étienne á Arnes on 25 June, followed by another on the 28th. He shot down a D VII the next day, and finished the month by burning the balloon at Rosières and attacking a second before jammed guns and engine trouble forced him to disengage. Bourjade teamed up with two squadronmates to destroy a balloon on 5 July and burned one solo on the 8th.

Bourjade eliminated three *Drachen* on 15 July, when the Germans launched their final assault across the Marne. Two days later he flamed

Lt Léon Jean-Pierre Bourjade was the top-scoring French balloon specialist, some 27 of his 28 victories being gasbags. He claimed that he was motivated by revenge for the artillery barrages balloon observers had called down upon him and his comrades when he was an infantryman (*SHAA B87.1781*)

another north of Nauroy and escaped an enemy fighter patrol with his SPAD riddled. His guns jammed and he was wounded in the arm while attacking a balloon near Tahure on 19 July, but he continued diving as it was winched down and at an altitude of just 300 metres he finally cleared his weapons and set it alight.

After three weeks in hospital and eight days' leave to visit his parents, Bourjade teamed up with Sous-Lt Ernest Joseph Jules Maunoury to destroy balloons on 30 August and 1 September. Three days later, he, Maunoury and Cpl Étienne Manson flamed another, and on 15 September he and Maunoury burned two more. Bourjade shared another two 'saucisses' with Maunoury over Orainville on 1 October, and he teamed up with other SPA152 pilots to burn balloons on 3, 4, 8 and 27 October.

Bourjade's diary entry for 29 October recorded his last victories – and the loss of a friend;

'In the Serancourt region I flamed a balloon at 1100 hrs. I destroyed another at 1125hrs, protected by (Sous-Lt Henri) Garin and (Sgt Gerard) Fos. In the afternoon I had two combats with Fokkers, with uncertain results. Had to break off, myself. At 1550 hrs Garin attacked a balloon at low altitude. When returning, I fought off a patrol of four or five Fokkers. At 1620 hrs, we met five other Fokkers. I attacked one, but the guns stopped immediately. After me, another SPAD attacked. I saw it above the enemy and closing in. At that moment it exploded and fell in the St Fergeux region. It was the SPAD piloted by Garin.'

Henri Garin, a fellow student for the priesthood who had shared in four of Bourjade's balloon victories, was credited to Oblt Robert Hildebrandt of Jasta 53.

By the time of the Armistice, Bourjade was credited with one enemy fighter and 27 balloons. He was made an Officier de la Légion d'Honneur, and also received the Croix de Guerre with 17 palmes and one étoile de vermeil. After finally attaining the priesthood on 26 July 1921, Bourjade served at a leper colony on Yui Island in British New Guinea, but in October 1924 he fell ill, and died on the 22nd of that month.

MdL Desiré Augustin Ducornet of SPA93 peers from the cockpit of his SPAD VII in the winter of 1918. Five of his seven victories were over balloons (Charles G Grey album via Jon Guttman)

Born at La Coucourde-Montelimar on 10 May 1910, Capitaine Fernand Bonneton had been a cavalry and infantry veteran, wounded four times, prior to his transferring to aviation in May 1916. Sent to Rumania in the spring of 1917, he scored his first two aerial victories there on 8 August and 30 October 1917. In May 1918, Bonneton returned to France and joined SPA69, with which squadron he downed an enemy aeroplane on 10 July, followed by balloons on 1, 15 and 22 August, the latter of which he flew through as it exploded in flames. He added more Drachen to his score on 2 September and 22 October, and survived the war with nine victories, the *Légion d'Honneur* and five foreign decorations. Bonneton commanded a squadron in Poland after the armistice, but on 24 June 1922 he was killed in a flying accident in Brussels, Belgium, while serving as commandant of the 1*e Groupe de Chasse*.

Other French balloon specialists included MdL Pierre Desiré Augustin Ducornet of SPA93, who in addition to a Pfalz on 29 May and a Rumpler on 15 July 1918, destroyed five balloons between 9 August and 29 September. In contrast to the 20-year-old Ducornet, pre-war aviator Adjutant-Chef Antoine Laplasse was 34 when he joined SPA75 on 20 October 1917, but he downed German two-seaters on 15 December 1917 and 13 March 1918, followed by a balloon on 18 June and two more on 17 August. With four squadronmates flying top cover, Laplasse burned three *Drachen* near Saint-Gobain on 22 August, and was going after a fourth when five D VIIs suddenly plunged through his flight, killing Sgt Jean Gentil and then sending Laplasse down in flames. Laplasse may have been the victim of Vzfw Hermann Korsch of *Jasta* 53.

Lt Charles Nungesser of SPA65 had already accounted for three *Drachen* in 1916 – his first at Septsarges on 2 April, the second during the mass effort of 22 May and a third on 26 September. His next such successes did not come until 1918, but they did so in one fearless flurry of activity on 14 August that saw his flame four balloons. The next day Nungesser shared in the destruction of an enemy aeroplane for his 43rd, and final victory, to become France's third-ranking ace.

While Nungesser was a renowned lone hunter, even working with what amounted to a 'roving commission', Armand Pinsard combined his vengeful pursuit of *'les Boches'* with a commander's responsibilities. Born in Nercillac on 28 May 1887, he was with MS23 when he was forced down in German lines on 8 February 1915. After 14 months, he and Capitaine Victor Menard escaped from the prison camp and made it back to French lines on 10 April 1916.

On 8 July Lt Pinsard reported to N26, commanded by Menard, and scored his first victory on 1 November. He was given command of N78 a short while later, and he downed a further 15 enemy aeroplanes with this unit before being injured in an accident on 12 June 1917. After several months in hospital, Pinsard returned to command his old unit, now

Having scored three balloon victories in 1916, Lt Charles Nungesser suddenly resumed that speciality with a vengeance in 1918, adding four more to his tally in a single sortie on 14 August (*N H Hauprich album via Jon Guttman*)

Lt Armand Pinsard of N78 poses with his SPAD VII, which featured a black fuselage and the personal motto *Revanche IV*, after scoring his ace-making fifth victory on 6 March 1917. Pinsard did not take up balloon-busting until after he took command of SPA23 in 1918, starting on 4 May and burning his ninth (for his 27th, and last, victory overall) on 22 August (*SHAA B96.1302*)

designated SPA23. He resumed his scoring on 20 February 1918, was awarded the British Military Cross on 17 April and burned his first *Drachen* on 4 May, followed by another on the 30th. A two-seater fell to Pinsard's guns on 6 June, then he commenced a balloon-busting streak, destroying *Drachen* on 8, 19 and 31 July, and 11, 14, 20 and 22 August.

With 18 aeroplanes and nine balloons to his credit, Capitaine Pinsard was made an *Officier de la Légion d'Honneur* on 30 August 1918, in addition to which he had the *Croix de Guerre* with 19 palms. Commanding GC21 in World War 2, Pinsard lost a leg after being wounded in a bombing raid on 6 June 1940. He died during a dinner held by the *Vieille Tiges* Association on 10 May 1953.

Arguably the ultimate embodiment of the balloon ace as the lone eccentric was the 'flying cowboy' who became the USAS's top-scoring balloon specialist. Born on 19 May 1897 and raised in Phoenix, Arizona, Frank Luke Jr was the son of a German immigrant from Westphalia who ruled his wife and children with an iron hand. Young Luke grew up resentful of authority, but he embraced the free environment of the West, becoming an accomplished horseman, a star athlete in school and a dead shot with the rifle and pistol. After the United States declared war on Germany, Luke eagerly enlisted in the Army Signal Corps on 27 September 1917. He found flight school a bore, but worked hard and proved to be a natural pilot.

During further training at the 3rd Aviation Instruction Centre at Issoudun, 2Lt Luke met the man whose name would soon be closely associated with his own. Born in Boston, Massachusetts, on 20 September 1895, Joseph Fritz Wehner was, like Luke, the son of a German immigrant, who after the United States entered the war frequently found himself under investigation as an enemy agent. Nothing came of it, save to leave Wehner bitter and distrustful of most company – the guileless Luke excepted.

On 30 May 1918 Luke was made a ferry pilot at the American Aviation Acceptance Park at Orly, but his irresponsible behaviour, combined with his insistence that he serve at the front, led his disgusted commander to accommodate him with a transfer to the 27th Aero Squadron of the 1st Pursuit Group, based at Touquin, on 26 July 1918. There, Luke's disrespect for the older pilots, while boasting of achievements he had yet to perform, alienated him from his squadronmates. Joe Wehner had joined the unit in June, however, leaving him with at least one friend, and the 27th's Canadian-born commander, Major Harold E Hartney, also perceived talent and potential in the unruly Arizonan.

On 16 August Hartney led 12 aircraft as an escort for a Salmson 2A2 of the 88th Aero Squadron, but the new SPAD XIIIs developed engine trouble and dropped out of formation one by one until only Hartney's and Luke's remained, and

2Lt Frank Luke Jr poses with a captured German Maxim machine gun before air and ground personnel of the 27th Aero Squadron at Rembercourt in September 1918. When he was not getting into trouble with his superiors, Luke spent much of his non-flying time practising his marksmanship (*Jon Guttman*)

A German Type AE kite balloon starts to catch fire after taking a sustained burst of incendiary bullets from an American SPAD XIII (*Jon Guttman*)

Lts Joseph F Wehner, Ivan A Roberts and William H Cosgrove (armaments officer) of the 27th Aero Squadron pose before Roberts' SPAD XIII '23'. Both Wehner and Roberts would be shot down while flying as Frank Luke's wingmen (*Jack Eder Collection via Jon Guttman*)

they became separated during a combat. When they returned to Touquin, Luke announced, 'I got a Hun', but his inability to provide further details precluded confirmation, and lowered the 'Arizona Boaster's' status to that of squadron pariah. Hartney took up the matter with his flight leaders, and 1Lt Jerry Vasconcells opined that Luke had potential. 'It isn't courage exactly. He has no imagination. He can't imagine anything happening to him. He thinks he's invincible. If he ever finds himself he may be almost as good as he thinks he is'.

Hartney kept Luke occupied flying solo patrols until 21 August, when he was promoted to command the 1st Pursuit Group. Capt Alfred A Grant took over the 27th, and tried to reimpose discipline on Luke – with predictably exasperating results. As a consequence of the 16 August mission, however, Luke typed up a set of confirmation forms to carry on future flights. Then, on the evening of 11 September, he overheard Vasconcells expressing his opinion of balloons. 'I think they're the toughest proposition a pilot has to meet. Any man who gets a balloon has my respect, because he's got to be good or he doesn't get it'.

The AEF launched its first offensive against the St Mihiel salient the next morning, and when the 27th sent up its first eight-aeroplane patrol, Luke dropped out to attack a German balloon at Marieville. After three passes, he sent it falling on its winch in flames. Although he landed near the frontlines to have US Army officers sign his confirmation sheet, official recognition of his first victory was delayed a few days. The Germans, however, knew what he had done. Bavarian observer Willy Klemm, who had just received his commission as leutnant that morning, died of wounds suffered in Luke's attack a few days later.

The real turning point in Luke's career occurred at 0930 hrs on the 14 September, when he and 1Lts Leo H Dawson and Thomas F Lennon burned a *Drachen* at Boinville. During a second sortie at 1430 hrs, Luke left his formation to destroy the balloon at Buzy. Eight D VIIs then attacked Luke, who suffered jammed guns, but Joe Wehner came to his aid, shooting down one Fokker and forcing another to land. Wehner then went after another of Bz 152's gasbags at Goin, only to see it destroyed by a French SPAD. The Frenchman, possibly MdL Aubailly of SPA153, came under attack by more Fokkers, but Wehner came to his rescue as well, driving down two of his assailants. Strangely, none of Wehner's victories for that day were confirmed.

On 15 September, Luke again dropped out of a patrol to destroy two balloons at Boinville. German fighters attacked and again Wehner saved him, this time being credited with a Fokker and an Albatros.

The following day Hartney and Grant invited Brig Gen William Mitchell to observe as Luke and Wehner carried out a scheduled raid on the German balloon line. The duo duly destroyed one at Reville at

41

1905 hrs, and after flak caused them to become separated, Luke burned a second *Drachen* at Romagne at 1920 hrs, while Wehner bagged a third over Mangiennes. Both of their SPADs required complete overhauls, but neither pilot suffered a scratch. General Mitchell described the action as 'one of the most remarkable feats in the military career of a youngster that was nothing short of amazing'.

Another witness was the 94th Aero Squadron's commander, 1Lt Eddie Rickenbacker, who noted a difference between the two aces. 'Luke would come back to the aerodrome and excitedly tell everyone about it, but no word would Wehner say on the subject. In fact Joe never spoke except in monosyllables on any subject. After a successful combat, he would put in the briefest possible report and sign his name'.

In only five days, the 'Arizona Boaster' and the suspected German spy from Boston had become the most talked-about phenomenon in the USAS. Sent out again on 18 September, they burned two German balloons near Labeuville, but were then attacked by enemy fighters. Luke sent two Fokkers crashing to earth and then, unable to find Wehner, flew east until he encountered an LVG that was being attacked by Sous-Lt Pierre Gaudermen and Adjutant Reginald Sinclaire of SPA.68. 'We spent two hours stalking that two-seater', Sinclaire recalled. 'After three attempts we finally cut him off. At the same time an American SPAD came up under his tail, also shooting, and landed where the German fell'.

The two Fokker pilots Luke brought down apparently survived, but the LVG crew of Ltns Ernst Höhne and Ernst Schulz of Fl. Abt. 36 were killed. Photographed beside the wreckage of his fifth victory in less than half an hour, Luke's face displayed both elation and concern that he expressed the next morning, when he asked Hartney, 'Wehner isn't back yet, is he, Major?' Mortally wounded by Ltn Georg von Hantelmann of *Jasta* 15, Luke's best friend died in a German field hospital.

Hartney ordered Luke to Orly Field – and nearby Paris – for eight days' leave, but he came back two days early and talked 2Lt Ivan A Roberts into joining him in an anti-balloon sortie on September 26. Fokkers attacked them en route, and although Luke drove one down out of control, Roberts was brought down by Ltn Franz Büchner of *Jasta* 13. He later escaped from prison, but died of fever near Wasselbonne on 14 October.

Upon returning, Luke wandered away without leave until 27 September – to be reprimanded by Grant, who added that soon after he had gone AWOL, the squadron had received a request to eliminate a balloon at Lisson. Unable to find Luke, Grant gave the job to Vasconcells, who destroyed it for his third victory.

On the 28th, Luke took off alone without filing a flight plan, destroyed a balloon in its nest at Banthéville and then spent the night with a nearby French balloon company. When he returned the next morning to hand in his combat report, Grant laid into him. 'See here, Luke. You're a good flier, one hell of a good flier, and you're also the damndest nuisance that ever stepped upon a flying field. But you're not running this outfit! Understand that? And you'll conform as the others do. You're on the ground until further notice. D'ya hear that?'

Soon after Luke left his office, however, Grant learned that he had flown to the 27th's auxiliary aerodrome near Verdun. Grant ordered Luke placed under arrest, declaring, 'I'm going to recommend him for the

Seen while still in training at Issoudun, in France, in the spring of 1918, 1Lt Joseph Wehner became Frank Luke's closest friend, as well as his 'top cover', when the duo teamed up to ravage the German balloon line in mid-September 1918 (*Jon Guttman*)

2Lt Frank Luke burned his first balloon on 12 September 1918, and by the 16th, he and his teammate Joe Wehner were the talk of the USAS. Luke is seen here with his Blériot-built SPAD XIII '26', which was just one of at least five fighters that he 'used up' within a week of braving gauntlets of flak and ground fire to add to his growing balloon tally (*Jon Guttman*)

Distinguished Flying Cross, then, by God, I'm going to court-martial him!'

In a last attempt at compromise between the 1st Pursuit's delinquent ace and his exasperated squadron leader, Hartney told Grant that Luke was slated to attack German balloons the next morning. On 29 September Luke departed Verdun, flew low over the 7th Balloon Company's headquarters at Souilly and dropped a message in a cylinder – 'Watch two German balloons at D-2 and D-4 positions – Luke.'

There are several accounts of what happened next, but all – including German records – confirm that Luke destroyed all three balloons as promised. As he burned the last *Drachen*, however, his SPAD was hit by its machine gun battery, commanded by Ltn Bernhard Mangels, and came down near Murvaux. French witnesses claimed that Luke strafed the German soldiers before finally landing 50 yards from a stream where, when called upon to surrender, he defiantly drew his pistol and died in the ensuing shootout.

After the war, however, Mangels – who somewhat ironically, hailed from Westphalia, from whence Luke's family had come – stated that Luke was dead when he and his men arrived at the scene, and that contrary to the 'ridiculous fairy tales' he had heard since, German troops did not abuse the body of *'Der fliegende Cowboy'*. The shots that the townspeople of Murvaux heard had likely been fired by an already wounded Luke to attract help, which arrived too late to save him from bleeding to death.

Luke never got his court martial, but he did receive a DSC with Oak Leaf Cluster, and soon after he became the first pilot in the USAS to be awarded the Medal of Honor, as well as a posthumous promotion to first lieutenant.

The career of the second-ranking American balloon ace roughly paralleled Luke's in some respects, but he was less of a disciplinary problem for the British squadron in which he briefly served – and far less famous. Born to a wealthy, politically prominent family in Weston, West Virginia, on 22 September 1894, Louis Bennett Jr grew up to be a likeable, but headstrong, young man, used to having his own way. Attending Yale, the muscular 5 ft 7 in-tall Bennett joined the university's lacrosse, crew, track and wrestling teams. Popular with the ladies, Bennett was also keen on mechanics, having his own automobile and motorcycle at age 12, and joining the Aero Club of America in 1916.

Early in March 1917 he got the idea of organising an air corps for his home state, which came to fruition in May when the governor authorised its formation, with a $10,000 grant. Based at Beech Bottom, near Wheeling, West Virginia, the West Virginia Flying Corps became official on 26 July, with Bennett among its first 15 cadets. Eventually it grew to

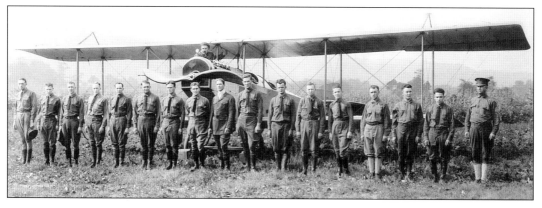

23 pilots and five Curtiss JN-4Ds before state funds ran out and the US Army Signal Corps refused to accept it as a military unit. Meanwhile, Bennett and his brother-in-law, Johnson C McKinley, established the West Virginia Aircraft Company, which license-built more than a million dollars' worth of engineless JN-4D airframes in 1917-18.

Eager to enter the war, Bennett completed his flight instruction at the Princeton Flying Club, and on 5 October 1917 he left for Toronto, Canada, hoping to join the RFC. After training in Texas and the Central Flying School at Upavon, England, he finally graduated on 6 March 1918, and was assigned to No 90 Sqn of what was now the RAF on 12 May. Initially flying Sopwith Dolphins in home defence, Bennett yearned for combat until he finally obtained a posting to SE 5a-equipped No 40 Sqn at Bryas on 21 July 1918. His commander, Maj Arthur W Keen, was an 'old hand' with 13 victories to his credit since 1916. The leader of 'C' Flight, to which Bennett was assigned, was Capt George Edward Henry McElroy, who was the war's leading Irish ace.

McElroy led Bennett on his first offensive patrol on 30 July, but they saw no action. Coming back from his second patrol the next day, however, Bennett wrote, 'My flight commander, Capt McElroy, on whom I was relying so much has, as the term goes "Gone West". He may be a prisoner, though no one saw him go down or in a fight'. After downing one more two-seater for his 49th victory, McElroy was killed in action, ironically credited to Vzfw Gullmann of *Jasta* 56 as his first, and only, success.

With Capt George C Dixon, a Canadian brought in from No 85 Sqn, taking over 'C' Flight, Bennett flew patrols from 4 through 11 August. Although No 40 Sqn had some successes – including a final victory for Maj Keen on the 9th – Bennett saw few aeroplanes, and on the several occasions when he spotted and went after enemy balloons, he failed to do much damage because his guns lacked Buckingham ammunition.

On 14 August Bennett wrote of finally receiving a regular aeroplane – Vickers-built SE 5a E3947, powered by a 200-hp Brasier Hispano engine. The next day, 'C' Flight dove on five Fokker D VIIs southwest of Douai and scattered them. 'I saw one scooting east', Bennett wrote, 'so dove to the left to head him off. Of course, my Vickers gun would not fire, so only got off half a drum of Lewis at him. I passed over him – a beautiful streamlined fuselage of a red chocolate colour. As I turned, he went into a spin and disappeared through the clouds'. A flightmate, Lt N D Willis, confirmed Bennett's first claim as 'out of control'.

Louis Bennett Jr is eighth from left in this line-up of pilots of the West Virginia Flying Corps, seen standing in front of a Curtiss JN-4D at Beech Bottom, West Virginia, in 1917. Bennett later flew SE 5as with No 40 Sqn, RAF, and was credited with three aeroplanes and nine balloons destroyed between 15 and 24 August 1918, when he was killed in action (*Otis L Reed*)

Maj Keen was badly burned in a flying accident on 15 August and Maj Robert J O Compston took command of No 40 Sqn on the 20th. Meanwhile, on 17 August, Bennett and Lt F H Knobel (another American squadronmate) downed an LVG two-seater east of Henin Lietard. Upon returning to Bryas, Bennett replenished his guns with Buckingham bullets and took off with Lt L H Sutton. East of Merville, they spotted a balloon at 2000 ft and Bennett broke away to dive at it. Holding his fire until he was close enough, he fired three-quarters of a Lewis drum into the *Drachen* and Sutton confirmed seeing it burst into flame. During the return flight, E3947 ran out of fuel and Bennett had to force land just short of his aerodrome.

Bennett now had 'the fever', writing to a friend that, 'Shooting down balloons is not so bad if you're a good bullet dodger'. 'He immediately set out to down every captive balloon in the area and we were all talking about it in the squadron', noted American squadronmate R A Anderson with some trepidation, 'each of us knew he was expendable.'

Oil problems delayed Bennett joining his patrol on 19 August. 'I saw them above me', he wrote, 'but was rather pessimistic about their finding anything, and as there were some Hun balloons out I went after them instead'. Diving from 11,000 to 2000 ft, he fired three-quarters of his Lewis drum into a *Drachen* east of Merville until it burst into flame. Spotting a second balloon at 1000 ft, Bennett ignored intense ground fire until he was near enough to empty his Lewis drum into the gasbag and see it burn, while the observer took to his parachute.

Landing at 1110 hrs and re-arming, Bennett flew back to Merville, and at 1340 hrs he spotted another balloon at 2000 ft. Diving in from the north, he managed to destroy that one as well. As he raced home at low altitude under continuous ground fire, he noticed yet another *Drachen* being winched down, and in spite of the German gunners being equally alerted to his presence, he fired a quarter of a drum of Lewis machine gun rounds into it before his weapon jammed. Concerned over failure during that first pass, Bennett looked back and was pleasantly surprised to see his target burning on the ground. He had become an ace within five days – and had destroyed four balloons in just three hours and forty minutes.

On the morning of 22 August, Nos 208 and 40 Sqns, escorted by Bristol Fighters of No 22 Sqn, raided Gondrecourt aerodrome, bombing and strafing hangars, machine gun emplacements and a nearby train. On the way back, the British destroyed four balloons, two of which fell to Bennett. Dixon led a dawn patrol the next day, during which he saw Bennett send an LVG crashing south of Quiery la Motte.

Low clouds marred the morning of 24 August, but when the weather improved later in the day, Bennett and fellow American 1Lt Reed G Landis volunteered for an offensive patrol at 1215 hrs. Landis suffered engine trouble, but Bennett carried on alone until he spotted a balloon at Provin and set it ablaze while its two occupants took to their parachutes. He then flew three miles northwest to Hantay, where he destroyed a second balloon.

Not far from Hantay, at a height of 1000 metres, German observer Emil Merkelbach saw the two *Drachen* go up in flames and ordered his crew to winch him down at once. 'I noticed that the enemy pilot was approaching my balloon at great speed', he later wrote, 'although our

45

heavy machine guns and anti-aircraft batteries were firing at him all the time. The aviator paid no attention, but continued to follow me. From a height of 50 metres he opened fire on my balloon. Fortunately, I was not hit, but the enemy aviator had been set afire through the attack of my machine guns. He attempted to rescue himself by jumping from the burning machine before it struck the earth. This brave and splendid aviator wore an identification plate marked "Louis Bennet Jr, Weston, W Va".'

SE 5a E3947 crashed near the station at Marquillas, one-and-a-half miles north of Hantay, the victim of Machine Gun Detachments Nrs 920 and 921. Impressed with the pilot's courage, the Germans burned their hands trying to extricate him from the wreckage, and stretcher bearers rushed him to their nearest field hospital at Wavrin. Bennett had a broken leg, a head wound and was badly burned from the waist to the neck. Madeline Dallène, a 20-year-old French girl pressed into German service as an assistant nursing orderly, recalled a doctor directing her to remove the American's boots, and hearing him call for his parents. He died before she could complete her instructions, and was buried with full military honours at the Wavrin German Military Cemetery.

Capt Dixon, in words rather reminiscent of Jerry Vasconcell's about Frank Luke, stated that Bennett 'feared absolutely nothing, and we wanted the greatest care taken of him until he mastered all the tricks of aerial fighting'. In spite of their concerns about his recklessness, his squadronmates – in contrast to Luke's – were unequivocal in their praise.

'Never had I seen such sterling work done in so short a time', wrote Maj Compston in a letter to Bennett's mother. 'He gave his whole heart to it. We shall miss him here, not only for his work, but for himself. I have recommended him for the Distinguished Flying Cross'. Strangely, he never received the medal. On 11 November 1925, however, an eight-foot bronze statue of him, designed by August Lukeman, was unveiled at the Linsly Military Institute at Wheeling, and Weston's Louis Bennett Public Library was named in his honour.

Balloon fever afflicted several German aces, too. As mentioned earlier, some budding specialists, such as Hans Heinrich Marwede, quickly fell victim to the hazards of the trade, but several enjoyed considerable success, and one unlikely character in the German ranks would set the wartime record of balloon kills in a single mission.

In at least one German case, 'balloon fever' was a passing fancy. Born in Gelsenkirchen, Westphalia, on 31 January 1892, Heinrich Bongartz had been a schoolteacher when war broke out, and he had gained his commission as an infantryman in March 1916, before completing flying training. After serving in two-seater units, he joined *Jasta* 36 in the spring of 1917 and scored his first victory on 6 April, when he brought down Lt Jean Mistarley of SPA31 in SPAD VII S244 – just after Mistarley had burnt a balloon at Lavannes. Bongartz soon took up balloon hunting himself, destroying two on 27 April, another two on 20 May and his fifth three days later.

After that, however, his victims were strictly heavier-than-air, totalling 33 before his Fokker Dr I (575/17) was shot down near Kemmel Hill by Capt C B McGlynn of No 74 Sqn. Bongartz survived the crash, but he suffered a debilitating head wound and lost his left eye. Wounded in the

Ltn Heinrich Bongartz underwent a short bout of 'balloon fever' in April-May 1917, burning five before sticking to aeroplanes for the bulk of his 33 victories (*Greg VanWyngarden*)

leg while fighting the Spartakists during Germany's post-war revolution, he subsequently became director of German air trade, dealing in airships. Bongartz died of a heart attack at Rheinberg on 23 January 1946.

Germany's first great balloon hunter was Heinrich Gontermann, who was born in Sigern, in southern Westphalia, on 25 February 1896. Joining the Army on 14 August 1914, he initially served in the 6th Uhlan Cavalry Regiment, with which he was wounded and commissioned in 1915. The end of the year saw him in the 80th Fusiliers, and applying for flight training. He subsequently served in *Kampfstaffel* Tergnier and Fl. Abt. 25, as both a pilot and observer as the mission required. Transferred to *Jasta* 5 on 11 November 1916, Gontermann shot down an FE 2b just three days later. His next success, over another FE 2b, did not occur until 6 March 1917, but he downed five more British aircraft between then and 6 April.

Gontermann destroyed his first balloon, belonging to the French 41*e Compagnie des Aérostiers*, west of St Quentin on 8 April. On the 13th he downed an FE 2d of No 57 Sqn over Vitry and a balloon of the 55*e Compagnie* southeast of St Quentin. A BE 2c fell to his guns the next day, and on the 16th Gontermann burned two British gasbags from the 14th Kite Balloon Section, 14th Company, 4th Wing (14-14-4) and from 6-15-4 at Manancourt, followed by one from 33-11-3 destroyed and another unconfirmed near Arras on the 22nd.

Although now a balloon ace, Gontermann did not go after them to the exclusion of other prey. He downed an RE 8 on 23 April, a Sopwith Triplane on the 24th and another British balloon, of 8-1-1, near Arras on the 26th. His performance during 'Bloody April' earned him the Iron Cross 1st Class and command of *Jasta* 15 in the French Aisne sector.

Gontermann spent his first few weeks with *Jasta* 15 adjusting to the responsibilities of leadership, although hardly from behind a desk. On 4 May he downed a SPAD VII, and two days later he accounted for another, killing Adjutant Célestin Eugène Jules Sanglier (a four-victory *Médaille Militaire* recipient) of *escadrille* N3 'Les Cigognes', and a Caudron R 4 that resulted in the death of C46's commander, and five-victory ace, Capitaine Didier Lecour-Grandmaison. That last double

Ltn Bongartz's Albatros D III 607/17 of *Jasta* 36, which allegedly had the name *Laura* painted on the left fuselage side below the cockpit (*Alex Imrie*)

Ltn Heinrich Gontermann with his Albatros D III D.2243/16 of *Jasta* 5, showing his black '2' that appeared on the fuselage sides and under both lower wings, and the stippled camouflage he applied to the fuselage and tail surfaces (*Greg VanWyngarden*)

47

Gontermann poses beside his Albatros D V while serving as *Staffelführer* of *Jasta* 15. Note that this aircraft also bore custom stippling, which was probably dark green over silver grey, on all upper surfaces, as well as a red band personal marking (*Greg VanWyndgarden*)

Ltn Hans Weiss gained all five of his balloon victories with *Jasta* 41 before going on to greater fame as a member of *Jagdgeschwader* I 'Richthofen'. His total victory claims came to 16, and he was put in command of *Jasta* 11 prior to his death in action on 2 May 1918 (*Greg VanWyngarden*)

Best known as the last CO of *Jagdgeschwader* II, Oblt Oskar von Boenigk scored his first five victories in *Jasta* 4, but did all his balloon-busting while serving in *Jasta* 21s, downing French gasbags on 4, 5 and 7 June, 16 and 24 July and 4 August 1918. He burned his seventh, from the 2nd US Balloon Company, south of Fismes on 7 August, and survived the war with a total of 26 victories (*Greg VanWyngarden*)

victory, along with another SPAD the next day, raised Gontermann's total to 21, for which he was awarded the *Orden Pour le Mérite* on the 14th. He also received the Knight's Cross with Swords on the Hohenzollern House Order on 6 May and the Bavarian Order of Max Josef on the 11th.

Gontermann evidently felt secure enough as *Staffelführer* to resume his balloon hunting sideline in June, starting with one from the *65e Compagnie* on the 24th and one from the *51e* three days later. He was credited with another French balloon on 16 July, a SPAD on the 24th and a Nieuport on 5 August. The latter month saw him reach his zenith, with double balloon victories on the 9th and 17th and a stellar performance on the 19th, in which he was credited with a SPAD southwest of Jouy at 1040 hrs and four balloons south of Aisne-Tal between 1923 and 1926 hrs. Gontermann downed a Caudron on 15 September, a SPAD and a Caudron on the 30th and another SPAD on 2 October.

Now one of Germany's leading fighter pilots, with 22 aeroplanes and 17 balloons to his credit, Gontermann was pleased to receive an early production specimen of Fokker's new Dr I (115/17) for frontline evaulation. On the afternoon of 30 October, soon after he had taken off in the reputedly fast-climbing and extremely nimble triplane on a test flight over *Jasta* 15's aerodrome at La Neuville, its upper wing suffered structural failure. Still alive when pulled from the wreckage, Gontermann died of his injuries soon after.

Jagdgeschwader I, the renowned Richthofen's 'Flying Circus', also boasted a few balloon specialists in its ranks, but most had attained that

status elsewhere. For example, Bavarian-born Hans Weiss had downed all five of his balloon victims while with *Jasta* 41 in 1917, prior to being made commander of *Jasta* 11, raising his total to 16 and being mortally wounded by Lt Merril Samuel Taylor of No 209 Sqn on 2 May 1918.

Oblt Oskar von Boenigk had downed five aeroplanes with *Jasta* 4 in 1917 prior to destroying seven balloons with *Jasta* 21 and assuming command of *Jagdgeschwader* II on 31 August 1918. He ended the war with a total of 26 victories to his credit. (*text continues on page 63*)

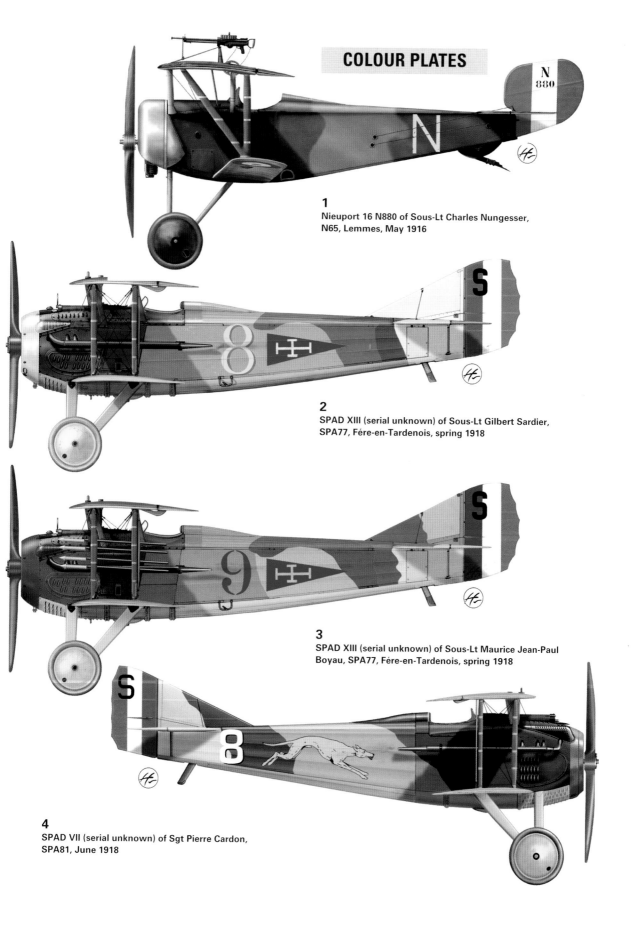

COLOUR PLATES

1
Nieuport 16 N880 of Sous-Lt Charles Nungesser,
N65, Lemmes, May 1916

2
SPAD XIII (serial unknown) of Sous-Lt Gilbert Sardier,
SPA77, Fére-en-Tardenois, spring 1918

3
SPAD XIII (serial unknown) of Sous-Lt Maurice Jean-Paul
Boyau, SPA77, Fére-en-Tardenois, spring 1918

4
SPAD VII (serial unknown) of Sgt Pierre Cardon,
SPA81, June 1918

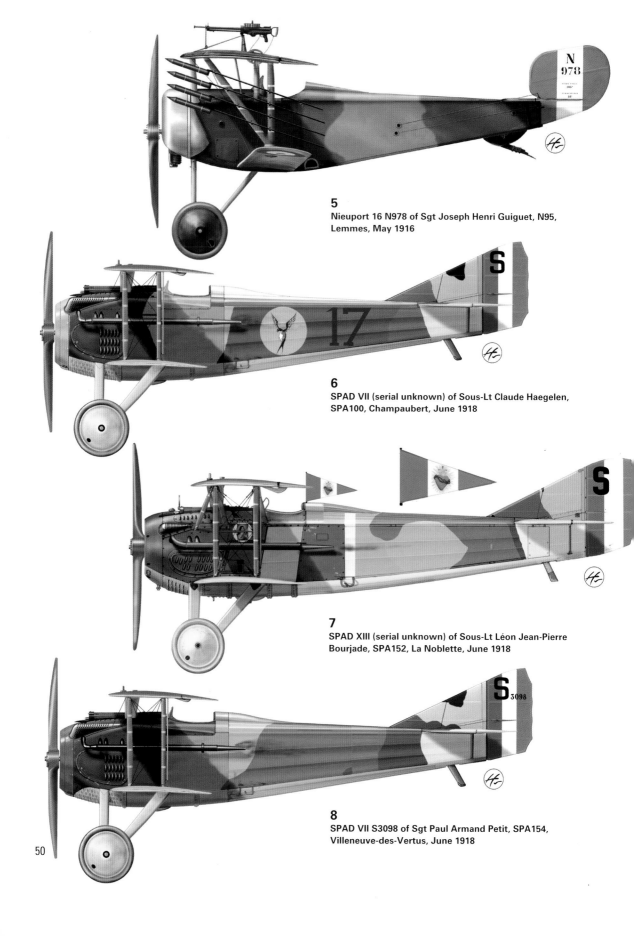

5
Nieuport 16 N978 of Sgt Joseph Henri Guiguet, N95,
Lemmes, May 1916

6
SPAD VII (serial unknown) of Sous-Lt Claude Haegelen,
SPA100, Champaubert, June 1918

7
SPAD XIII (serial unknown) of Sous-Lt Léon Jean-Pierre
Bourjade, SPA152, La Noblette, June 1918

8
SPAD VII S3098 of Sgt Paul Armand Petit, SPA154,
Villeneuve-des-Vertus, June 1918

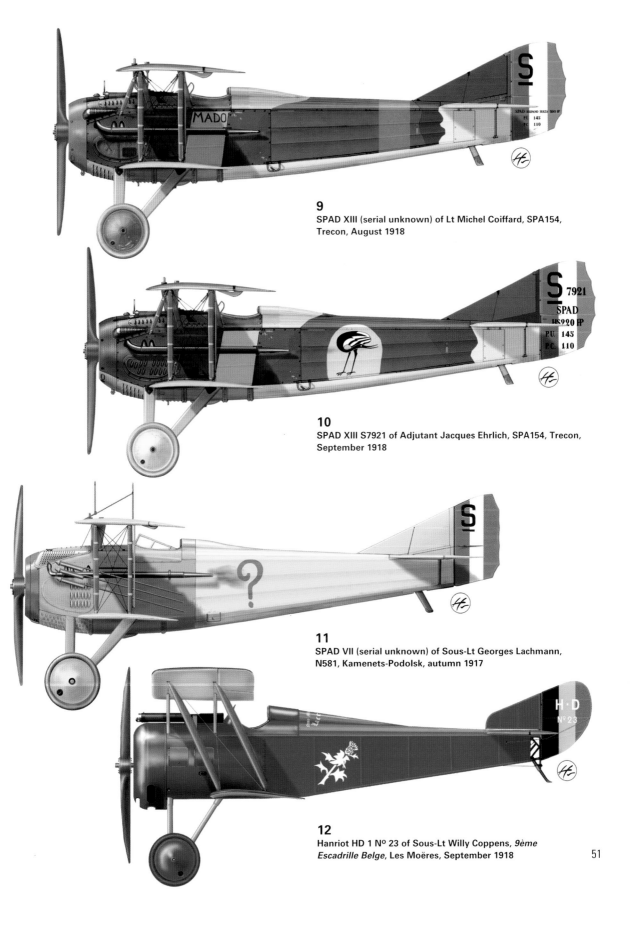

9
SPAD XIII (serial unknown) of Lt Michel Coiffard, SPA154,
Trecon, August 1918

10
SPAD XIII S7921 of Adjutant Jacques Ehrlich, SPA154, Trecon,
September 1918

11
SPAD VII (serial unknown) of Sous-Lt Georges Lachmann,
N581, Kamenets-Podolsk, autumn 1917

12
Hanriot HD 1 N° 23 of Sous-Lt Willy Coppens, *9ème
Escadrille Belge*, Les Moëres, September 1918

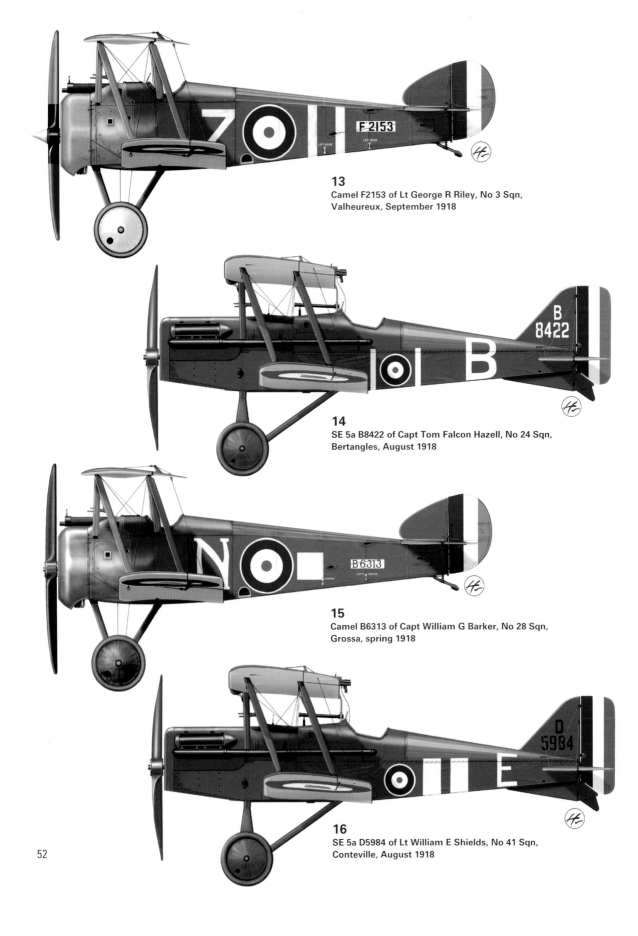

13
Camel F2153 of Lt George R Riley, No 3 Sqn,
Valheureux, September 1918

14
SE 5a B8422 of Capt Tom Falcon Hazell, No 24 Sqn,
Bertangles, August 1918

15
Camel B6313 of Capt William G Barker, No 28 Sqn,
Grossa, spring 1918

16
SE 5a D5984 of Lt William E Shields, No 41 Sqn,
Conteville, August 1918

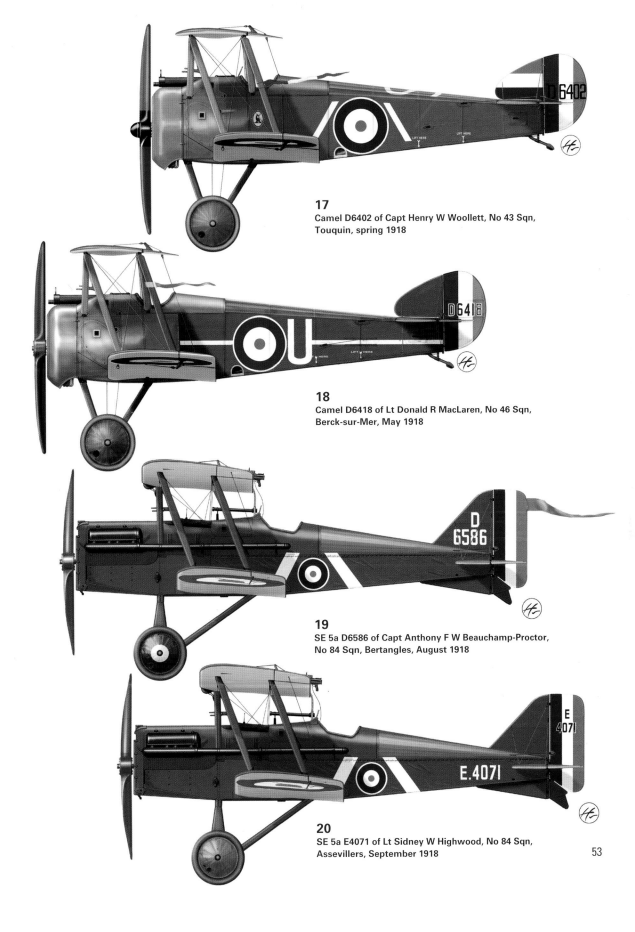

17
Camel D6402 of Capt Henry W Woollett, No 43 Sqn,
Touquin, spring 1918

18
Camel D6418 of Lt Donald R MacLaren, No 46 Sqn,
Berck-sur-Mer, May 1918

19
SE 5a D6586 of Capt Anthony F W Beauchamp-Proctor,
No 84 Sqn, Bertangles, August 1918

20
SE 5a E4071 of Lt Sidney W Highwood, No 84 Sqn,
Assevillers, September 1918

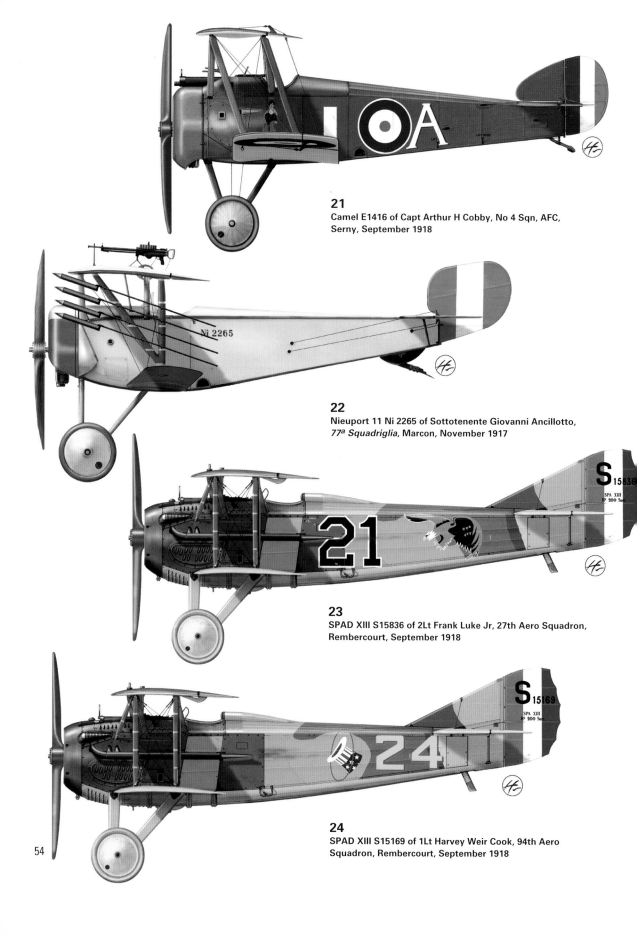

21
Camel E1416 of Capt Arthur H Cobby, No 4 Sqn, AFC,
Serny, September 1918

22
Nieuport 11 Ni 2265 of Sottotenente Giovanni Ancillotto,
77ª Squadriglia, Marcon, November 1917

23
SPAD XIII S15836 of 2Lt Frank Luke Jr, 27th Aero Squadron,
Rembercourt, September 1918

24
SPAD XIII S15169 of 1Lt Harvey Weir Cook, 94th Aero
Squadron, Rembercourt, September 1918

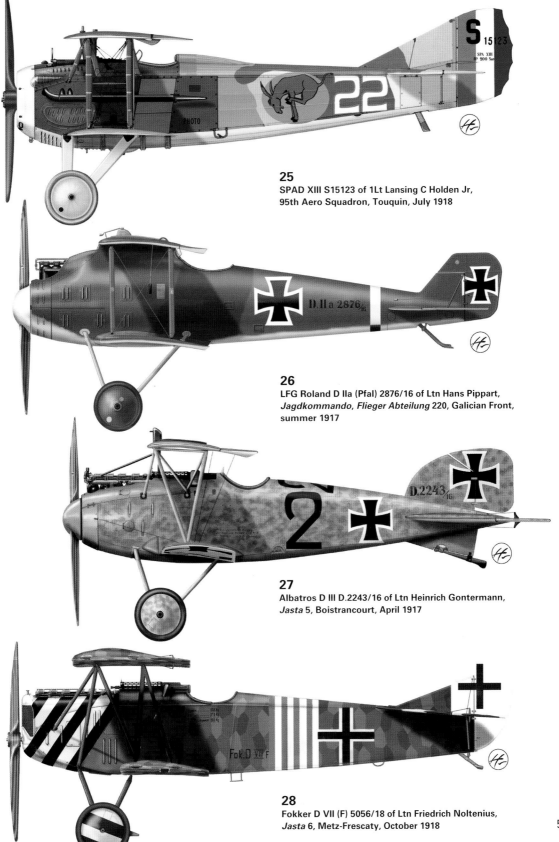

25
SPAD XIII S15123 of 1Lt Lansing C Holden Jr,
95th Aero Squadron, Touquin, July 1918

26
LFG Roland D IIa (Pfal) 2876/16 of Ltn Hans Pippart,
Jagdkommando, *Flieger Abteilung* 220, Galician Front,
summer 1917

27
Albatros D III D.2243/16 of Ltn Heinrich Gontermann,
Jasta 5, Boistrancourt, April 1917

28
Fokker D VII (F) 5056/18 of Ltn Friedrich Noltenius,
Jasta 6, Metz-Frescaty, October 1918

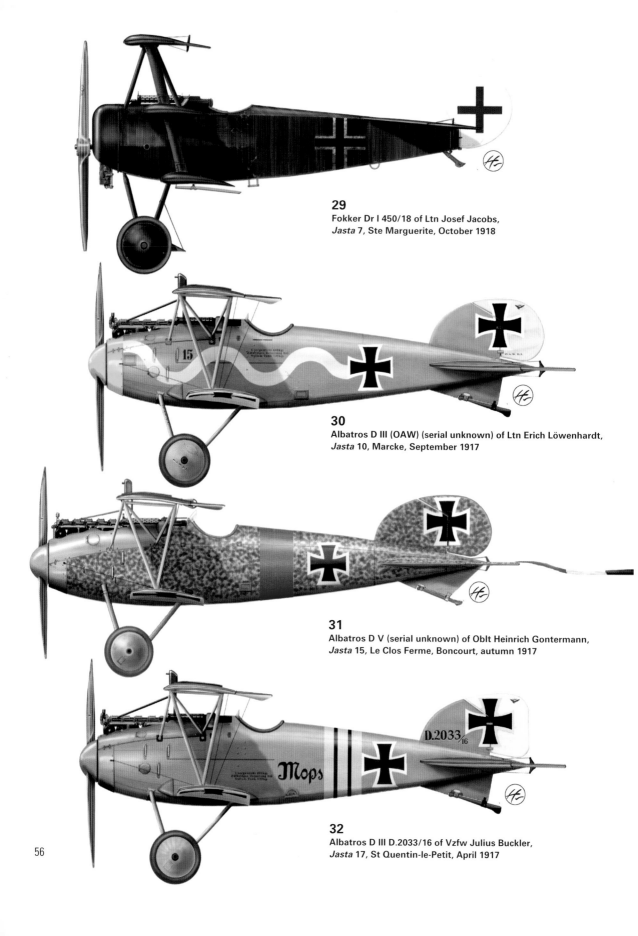

29
Fokker Dr I 450/18 of Ltn Josef Jacobs,
Jasta 7, Ste Marguerite, October 1918

30
Albatros D III (OAW) (serial unknown) of Ltn Erich Löwenhardt,
Jasta 10, Marcke, September 1917

31
Albatros D V (serial unknown) of Oblt Heinrich Gontermann,
Jasta 15, Le Clos Ferme, Boncourt, autumn 1917

32
Albatros D III D.2033/16 of Vzfw Julius Buckler,
Jasta 17, St Quentin-le-Petit, April 1917

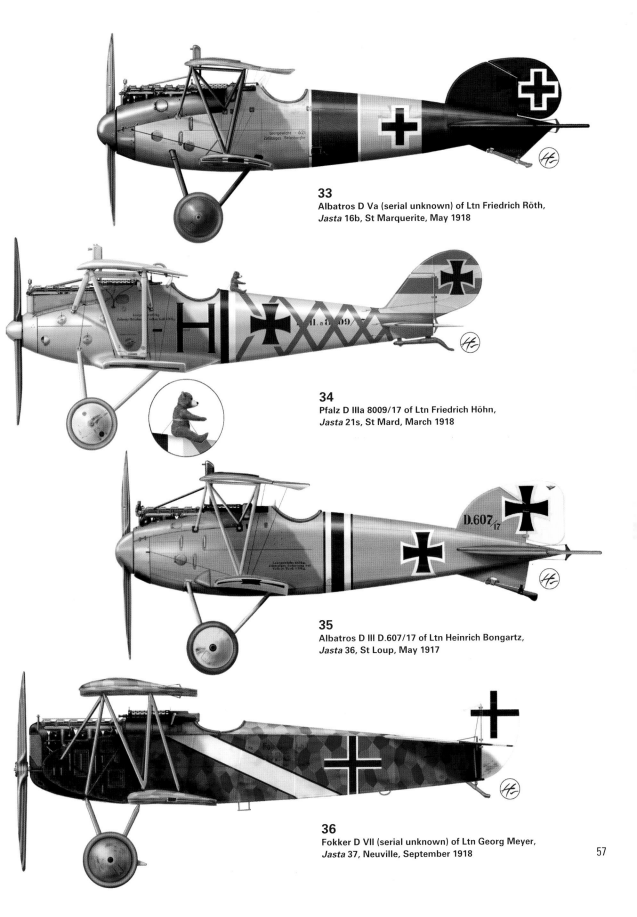

33
Albatros D Va (serial unknown) of Ltn Friedrich Röth,
Jasta 16b, St Marquerite, May 1918

34
Pfalz D IIIa 8009/17 of Ltn Friedrich Höhn,
Jasta 21s, St Mard, March 1918

35
Albatros D III D.607/17 of Ltn Heinrich Bongartz,
Jasta 36, St Loup, May 1917

36
Fokker D VII (serial unknown) of Ltn Georg Meyer,
Jasta 37, Neuville, September 1918

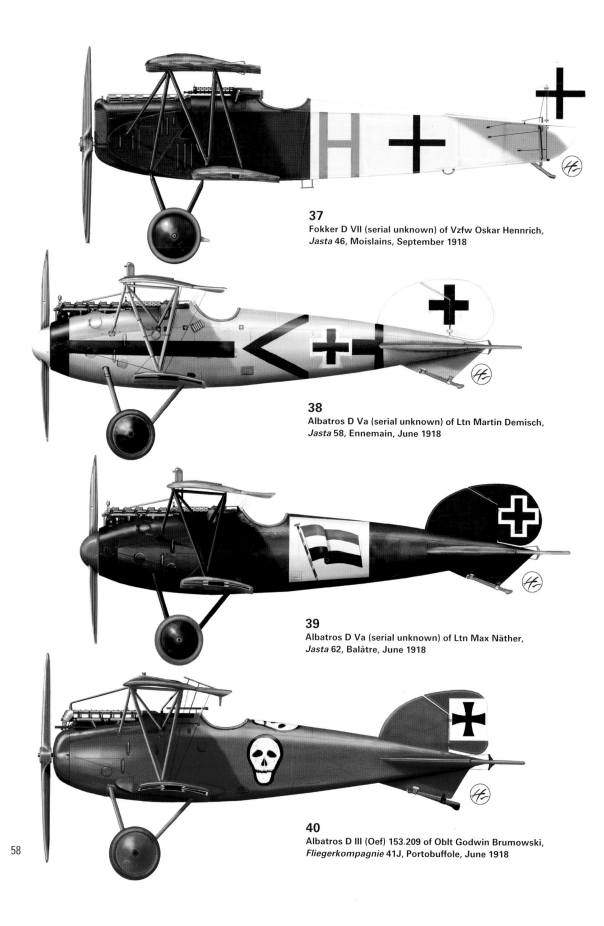

37
Fokker D VII (serial unknown) of Vzfw Oskar Hennrich,
Jasta 46, Moislains, September 1918

38
Albatros D Va (serial unknown) of Ltn Martin Demisch,
Jasta 58, Ennemain, June 1918

39
Albatros D Va (serial unknown) of Ltn Max Näther,
Jasta 62, Balâtre, June 1918

40
Albatros D III (Oef) 153.209 of Oblt Godwin Brumowski,
Fliegerkompagnie 41J, Portobuffole, June 1918

Planform 1
SPAD XIII (serial unknown) of Sous-Lt Gilbert Sardier,
SPA77, Fére-en-Tardenois, spring 1918

Planform 2
SPAD VII (serial unknown) of Sous-Lt Claude Haegelen,
SPA100, Champaubert, June 1918

Planform 3
SE 5a D5984 of Lt William E Shields, No 41 Sqn,
Conteville, August 1918

Planform 4
Camel D6418 of Lt Donald R MacLaren, No 46 Sqn,
Berck-sur-Mer, May 1918

Planform 5
SPAD XIII S15123 of 1Lt Lansing C Holden Jr,
95th Aero Squadron, Touquin, July 1918

Planform 6
Albatros D III (OAW) (serial unknown) of Ltn Erich
Löwenhardt, *Jasta* 10, Marcke, September 1917

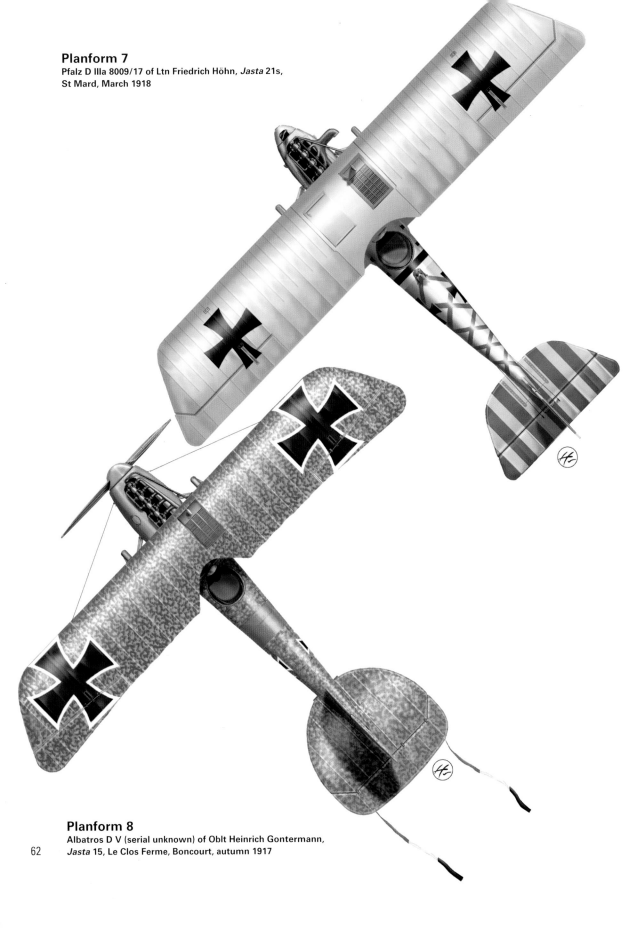

Planform 7
Pfalz D IIIa 8009/17 of Ltn Friedrich Höhn, *Jasta* 21s,
St Mard, March 1918

Planform 8
Albatros D V (serial unknown) of Oblt Heinrich Gontermann,
Jasta 15, Le Clos Ferme, Boncourt, autumn 1917

Oblt Hans Klein was credited with 11 aeroplanes and five balloons destroyed with *Jasta* 4 before being wounded on 13 July 1917. He was subsequently given command of *Jasta* 10 on 27 September, with whom he downed five more aeroplanes and burned one more balloon (of 41-15-3) west of Cambrai on 30 November. Klein received the *Orden Pour le Mérite* on 2 December, but he lost his right thumb in a scrap with Camels of No 54 Sqn on 19 February 1918 and spent the rest of the war as a ground officer in *Jasta* 10. Klein rose to major general and deputy commander of fighters in the *Luftwaffe* during World War 2, before dying on 18 November 1944.

Ltn d R Friedrich Theodor Noltenius burned his first four British balloons with *Jasta* 27, including one near Vitry-en-Artois on 14 September 1918, of which he commented;

'I only wanted to press the attack home when suddenly, while I was a mere 50 metres away, a gigantic flame rose which completely engulfed me! The shock hurled me away. I at once took course for the lines after I had discovered that the machine was still in flying condition. But what a shambles she was! The cloth covering had become completely slack all over the machine and billowed. Large shreds of balloon cloth hung in the struts and in the empennage. The controls acted perfectly different. To movements of the rudder, the aeroplane did not react at all. In addition, it was excessively tail-heavy. In this condition I would have been unable to survive in a dogfight. Fortunately, the strong western wind carried me home to our lines very quickly and I was able to land safely on our field.'

On 27 September Noltenius transferred to *Jasta* 6 of JG I, and on 6 October he burned a gasbag of the US Army's 10th Balloon Company. A quarrel with his *Staffelführer*, Ltn Ulrich Neckel, compelled Noltenius to transfer again, to *Jasta* 11, on 19 October. Four days later he burned a gasbag of the US 5th Balloon Company, downed a SPAD XIII in Allied lines (whose LFC pilot Sgt Edwin B Fairchild of SPA159, survived) and finished the day by frying another 'sausage' of the 2nd Balloon Company. A final victim from the 8th Balloon Company on 28 October was followed by Liberty DH 4 bombers on 3 and 4 November to bring the Bremen-born Noltenius' final tally to 21.

Appointed *Staffelführer* of *Jasta* 10 following Ltn Werner Voss' death on 23 September 1917, Ltn Hans Klein destroyed his sixth balloon (and 22nd victory overall) on 30 November, and was awarded the *Orden Pour le Mérite* two days later (*Jon Guttman*)

Ltn Friedrich Noltenius' *Jasta* 27 Fokker D VII looks like it has seen decidedly better days after returning from his anti-balloon sortie of 14 September 1918. The red and white bands, representing Noltenius' hometown of Bremen, also appeared on the fuselage of his later *Jasta* 6 D VII, but not on the upper wing as per *Jasta* 27 practice (*Greg VanWyngarden*)

This line-up of yellow-nosed Pfalz D IIIs of *Jasta* 10 at Marke in November 1917 includes Ltn Hans Klein's machine, with the horizontal fuselage stripe, fifth from left (*Jon Guttman*)

Attaining that score too late to receive the *Orden Pour le Mérite*, Noltenius was one of the last recipients of the Knight's Cross of the Royal Hohenzollern House Order, on 8 November 1918. Becoming a doctor after the war, Noltenius resumed flying, but as he took off from Johannisthal Airport on 12 March 1936, his Bücker Jungmann crashed and he died of his injuries en route to the hospital.

The star balloon specialist of the 'Flying Circus' was Friedrich 'Fritz' Friedrichs, who was born in Spark, Westphalia, on 21 February 1895. Planning on being a doctor before war broke out, he served in France with the 85th Infantry Regiment, but later got his commission while fighting Serbs with the 32nd Infantry in the Balkans. Wounded and classified unfit for the infantry, 'Fritz' trained as an observer and then a pilot in 1917. After earning the Iron Cross 1st and 2nd Class in Fl. Abt.(A) 264, he joined *Jasta* 10 of JG I on 11 January 1918.

Friedrich's first claim (a Camel on 18 March) went unconfirmed, but he officially opened his account with a balloon on the 21st. His next three victories were over aircraft, but on 18 May he inaugurated a balloon-busting spree with a British gasbag of 35-12-3 over Ransart, followed by one south of Chavigny ten days later. On 5 June he downed two balloons north of Villers Cotterets, and added more on the 6th and 8th. After

Eight of the twenty-one victories Ltn Friedrich Noltenius scored with *Jasta*s 27, 6 and 11 were over balloons. The war ended and the Kaiser had abdicated before the ace could receive a well-deserved *Orden Pour le Mérite* (*Jon Guttman*)

Ltn Friedrich 'Fritz' Friedrichs is seen in a Pfalz D III of *Jasta* 10. The 11 balloons among his 21 victories made him the leading balloon ace of the Richthofen's 'Flying Circus', but an unfortunate succession of circumstances brought his career to an untimely end on 15 July 1918 (*Greg VanWyngarden*)

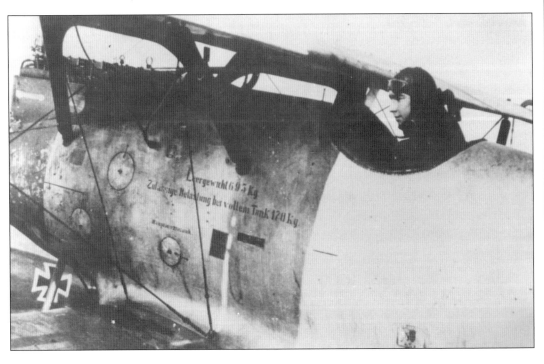

downing a Breguet 14 on the 9th, Friedrichs destroyed a balloon on the 16th, a SPAD on the 23rd and another balloon on the 25th. Two SPADs fell to his guns on the 27th, a third on the 28th and he finished the month with a double balloon victory on the 30th, eliminating the 43e *Compagniea 'saucisse'* over Fleury and the 54e's over Château Thierry.

Friedrichs' last victories were Nieuport 28s of the American 1st Pursuit Group on 2 and 8 July. On the 15th his Fokker D VII 309/18 suddenly caught fire, which was subsequently attributed to sponaneous combustion of his incendiary ammunition in the July heat within the poorly ventilated cowling, causing an explosion that set his fuel tank ablaze. Friedrichs bailed out, but his parachute caught and ripped on his tailplane. With 21 victories (ten of which were over balloons), 'Fritz' Friedrichs had been recommended for the *Orden Pour le Mérite*, but it was announced five days after his death.

One of Germany's most fearless balloon specialists never received the *Pour le Mérite* because he was not a commissioned officer. Starting his career as a gunner with *Kampfgeschwader* 2 between 20 April 1916 and 20 February 1917, Oskar Hennrich subsequently trained to be a pilot in Fl. Abt.(A) 273 from 10 October 1917 to 6 May 1918, when he transferred to *Jasta* 46. There, Vzfw Hennrich came into his own, burning a British balloon of 1-18-3 west of Albert on 14 May, downing a Camel southeast of Albert on the 18th and claiming two balloons northwest of Albert – one of which was confirmed – on the 29th.

After downing an RE 8 on 30 July, Hennrich scored a double balloon victory on 1 August – 43-15-5's southwest of Bonnay and 29-12-5's at Daours – followed by an SE 5a on the 8th, a Camel on the 9th, 12-16-5's balloon near Marcelcave on the 18th, and another gasbag, from 1-18-3, west of Albert on the 25th. During that month *Jasta* 46 traded its Albatros D Va and Pfalz D IIIa fighters for Fokker D VIIs, and after downing an SE 5a on 3 September, Hennrich resumed his balloon spree, burning 14-4-5's gasbag south of Le Mesnil on the 6th, 44-19-5's at Bertincourt on the 15th, and being credited with a 'hat trick' on the 24th, although British records only acknowledge two – 31-18-3's burned between Etricourt and Manoncourt and 1-18-3's at Fins.

Hennrich finished September with another British balloon (6-15-5's at Lieramont) on the 26th, a Bristol Fighter of No 22 Sqn on the 27th, an SE 5a on the 29th and 31-18-3's balloon at Gouzeaucourt on 1 October. Of the 18 to 20 victories credited to Hennrich, 13 were balloons. Although denied Prussia's highest honour for officers, *Jasta* 46's enlisted hero was awarded the Golden Military Merit Cross on 3 November 1918 and survived the war.

Less fortunate was Karl Paul Schlegel. Born in Wechselburg, Saxony, on 7 May 1893, he attended military schools and had served in Royal Sachsenberg Machine gun Sections Nr 19 and 8 before the war. He saw action in France and Russia with the 8th Cavalry Division, but he tired of trench warfare and took flight training in the spring of 1917. Schlegel began frontline service in Fl. Abt. 39, but was soon injured in a crash.

After fighter training in January 1918, Uffz Schlegel was assigned to *Kampfeinsitzer Staffel* 1 in May, although five days later he was reassigned to *Jasta* 45. There, he found his calling when he destroyed a balloon at Villers Cotterets on 14 June. Schlegel followed that up by 'roasting' the

Vzfw Oskar Hennrich sports a captured pair of cut-down fur-lined British 'fug boots', which were a much-prized item, beside his Fokker D VII of *Jasta* 46. Thirteen of his twenty victories were over balloons (*Jon Guttman*)

French 45*e Compagnie's 'saucisse'* over Comblizy on 4 July and destroying another from the US 2nd Balloon Company two days later. SPADs fell to his guns on 15 July, when he was also promoted to vizefeldwebel. Schlegel went on to burn French balloons on the 19th and 20th, downed a Breguet 14 on the 22nd, and destroyed a Breguet and a balloon on the 25th. He claimed more Breguets on 29 and 30 July and a SPAD XI on 4 August.

Schlegel's next victim was from the US 1st Balloon Company on 6 August, followed by two more gasbags on the 12th, another two on the 21st – at the expense of the 33*e* and 83*e Compagnie*s – and a SPAD on the 29th. Schlegel added a balloon of the 29*e Compagnie* to his score over Ouilly on 1 September, another from the 26*e* at Sarcy on the 4th. His 14th balloon at Fismes the next day was also his 22nd victory overall.

On 27 October Schlegel ventured over the lines and the German records refer to his having downed a balloon and a SPAD XI at La Malmaison, before being shot down in a fight with 12 French aircraft, although neither victory was confirmed. The French noted that he was killed after attacking a balloon near Amilfontaine at 1540 hrs, being credited to Sous-Lt Pierre Marinovitch of SPA94 as his 19th victory.

Like Heinrich Gontermann, Germany's youngest balloon ace divided his time between lone forays and the responsibilities of command. Born in Tepliwoda, East Prussia, on 24 August 1899, Max Näther enlisted in the infantry at just 15, was commissioned a leutnant on 11 August 1916 and after pilot training, joined *Jasta* 62 on 31 March 1918. Downing a SPAD XIII on 16 May, he scored a succession of victories over French balloons on 1, 5, 7, 16, 27 and 28 June. Soon after downing a Sopwith Dolphin for his eighth victory Näther, still only aged 18, was given command of his *Staffel* on 7 July.

Flying Fokker D VIIs, he brought his total to 26 – including another French and three American balloons. After burning the 7th Balloon Company's gasbag over Cierges on 23 October, his Fokker was apparently pursued by 1Lt Jacques Swaab of the 22nd Aero Squadron, who was credited with sending the Fokker crashing into German lines in flames, although Näther in fact survived. He was recommended for the *Orden Pour le Mérite*, but the imperial government collapsed before it could be approved. While fighting in Germany's border war with Poland, Näther was shot down and killed by ground fire near Kolmar, Schlesien, on 8 January 1919.

The man destined to be Germany's leading balloon ace, Friedrich Röth, was born the son of a factory owner in Nuremberg on 29 September 1893. 'Fritz' was just graduating from college when war broke out and he promptly enlisted

The youngest German balloon ace, Ltn Max Näther claimed ten gasbags destroyed in his final tally of 26 victories (*Norman Franks*)

Ltn Friedrich Höhn of *Jasta* 21s (right) poses with visiting Ltn Müller of Fl. Abt.(A) 274 beside his Pfalz D IIIa 8009/17 at St Mard in the spring of 1918. 'Fritz' Höhn had 21 victories, including ten balloons, to his credit when he was mortally wounded on 3 October 1918 (*Greg VanWyngarden*)

in *Feldartillerie Regiment Nr 6*. He went to the front on 6 September 1914, and soon after being promoted to unteroffizier, was severely wounded. After recovering, Röth volunteered for the *Luftstreitskräfte* in early 1916, managing to qualify as a pilot in spite of defective eyesight.

Posted to Fl. Abt.(A) 296 on 1 April 1917, he was awarded the Bavarian Military Merit Order 4th Class with Swords on 11 June and, after training as a fighter pilot, newly commissioned Ltn d R Röth joined Bavarian *Jasta* 23b at St Mard aerodrome, in the Verdun sector, on 4 October.

Ltn Friedrich Röth sits in the cockpit while his OAW-built Albatros D Va undergoes engine maintenance at *Jasta* 23b's aerodrome at Puseiux in January 1918. On 25 January 'Fritz' Röth began his scoring with a 'hat trick' of French balloons in just eight minutes (*Jon Guttman*)

'Röth was not a braggart nor a rough fighter by nature', *Jasta* 23b squadronmate Max Gossner later said of him, 'but was mild, gentle, human and an idealist in the truest sense. A soldier, an officer of unusually hight devotion to duty and possessing the courage of a daredevil'. Although he was a steadfast wingman, for which he received the Iron Cross 1st Class on 1 November 1917, Röth's faulty eyesight made for an unproductive three months until he decided to engage enemy aeroplanes at pointblank range, and to volunteer to attack balloons, which despite the hazards involved, offered nice, large targets once he got to them.

On 25 January 1918, while *Jasta* 23b's commander Ltn d R Otto Kissenberth was bringing down a SPAD over Montfaucon – mortally wounding LFC volunteer Cpl Philip R. Benney of SPA67 – Röth was flying deep into French *IIe Armée* territory. All hell broke loose at 1300 hrs when Röth burned the balloon of the 55*e Compagnie* at Recicourt and its occupants, MdL A Bretonache and Sgt A Guquère, took to their parachutes. Elated at his good luck, Röth decided to push it a bit farther by attacking the 59*e Compagnie's* balloon over Bethelaincourt, forcing Lt L Bigot to bail out as his platform, too, descended in a mass of flames.

Minutes later, Röth appeared over Framèreville, where the 80*e Compagnie,* alerted by the smoke from his first victim, had winched its balloon down to 60 metres when Röth dove through a hail of ground fire to burn that, too. In spite of the low altitude, one French aeronaut managed to parachute down safely, but the other, MdL T Faure, was killed. At 1308 hrs, Röth's bullet-riddled Albatros D Va finally alighted at St Mard, where its weary pilot received his *Staffelführer's* hearty congratulations.

Oblt Otto Schmidt, commander of *Jasta* 5, stands in front of a Fokker D VII in the autumn of 1918. Born in Neukirchen on 23 March 1885, Schmidt had previously downed six balloons and four aeroplanes while serving with Fl. Abt. 25 and *Jastas* 7, 32 and 29. He doubled that score with *Jasta* 5, including a balloon south of Morcourt on 26 August and another southwest of Bertincourt on 7 September 1918 (*Jon Guttman*)

On 4 February 1918 *Jasta* 23b left St Mard to join *Jastas* 35b, 58 and 59 in *Jagdgruppe* 4 at Aniche, in the 17. *Armee* sector. There, they were to support General Erich Ludendorff's coming offensive against the British. On 26 February a point-blank attack on an RE 8 east of Arleux gained Röth his fourth victory. On 15 March *Jagdgruppe* 4 was dissolved and *Jagdgruppe* 9 formed around *Jastas* 23b, 32b, 35b and 59. *Jasta* 23b moved to Emerchicourt aerodrome the next day.

Jagdgruppe **8 commander Hptm Eduard Ritter von Schleich poses between two of his** *Staffelführer,* **with a Roland D VI in the background, during a visit to** *Jasta* **23b's field at Epinoy in the spring of 1918.** *Jasta* **23b's Oblt Otto Kissenberth holds Ltn Theodor Rumpel's dachshund at left, while Ltn 'Fritz' Röth, commander of** *Jasta* **16b, smiles at right (***Jon Guttman***)**

The final German push on the Western Front commenced on 21 March, with the elimination of British balloons observing the 17. *Armee* among the German fighters' vital tasks. Röth eagerly volunteered, and at 1130 hrs he burned one from 44-19-3 at Marcoing, whose observer, 2Lt A M Burton, parachuted safely. Five minutes later, Röth sent a second balloon, of 1-18-3, up in flames north of Beugny.

On 24 March *Jasta* 23b moved up to Epinoy. On 1 April, while the RFC and RNAS were being amalgamated into the RAF, Röth began an unprecedented 'sausage roast' in the 1st Balloon Wing's sector at 1730 hrs, with the destruction of 10-2-1's gasbag at Cambrin. Four minutes later he burned 8-1-1's balloon over Hulloch, followed by the 20-1-1's over Loos at 1736 hrs and 24-2-1's south of Loos just two minutes later.

Röth's score now stood at ten, but his lone-wolf forays were soon tempered by the responsibilities of leadership. On 29 April he was promoted to oberleutnant and transferred to St Marguerite to take command of *Jasta* 16b, whose previous *Staffelführer*, Ltn Heinrich Geigl, had been killed on the 4th in a mid-air collision with a Camel flown by Lt J G Kennedy of No 65 Sqn.

Röth added nothing to *Jasta* 16b's bag over the next month, but one of its members, former Pfalz test pilot Uffz Max Holtzem, remembered his activities during May 1918;

'He studied the balloon situation at Ypres for awhile. Early each morning, before we came out, he was standing beside his ready Albatros D V, at the telescope. On 29 May, there was a long line of ten observation balloons up, in a line diagonal to the front at Ypres where the frontline forms a kneebend. He went up alone, not waiting for us, and coming in from the east, shot down five balloons in flames. It all happened so fast that although we had taken off right after him, and saw it from above, when we came home he was already there and safe. His ship was hit by machine-gun fire and AA shrapnel right through a wing, and his barograph, which hung underneath his seat, was smashed.'

Röth wrote his own account of the action;

'On 29 May 1918, I saw from our airfield, at about 1500 hrs, ten English captive balloons already high up. It had been three weeks since I had attacked the balloon row on this front, and this was the first afternoon that the conditions were favourable. The English fighter squadrons were not to be seen – only some small utility aircraft flying from time to time over the front. I started along around 1530 hrs and flew against the wind towards Wervicq and Roulers.

'South of Dixmuide, I was at 2000 metres over English territory. The strong northwest wind would be to my advantage on my return. In the raging defensive fire of English ground machine guns, I shot down three

Another German who divided his efforts between lone balloon-busting and leadership was Ltn Josef Carl Peter Jacobs, shown here beside one of at least two Clerget-powered Fokker Dr Is that he flew while commanding *Jasta* 7 at Ste Marguerite. Eight of Jacobs' 41 victories were over balloons (*Greg VanWyngarden*)

captive balloons in flames between Dixmuide and Poperinghe and two between Poperinghe and Hazebrouck. Shortly after shooting down the third, I was attacked myself, southwest of Poperinghe, by an aircraft with French cockades – probably a SPAD. I diverted his attack with a counter curve. As he tried to get behind me, I got behind him and he went into the frightened right curve. I got the advantage, but could not overtake the SPAD.

'Three English aeroplanes were now coming at me from the directon of Bailleul. I therefore made my attack on two balloons that were still high up, northeast of Hazebrouck, and with extreme speed turned and came out over Merville and returned to our lines.

'Between the separate attacks on the captive balloons I was at a height of 500 to 1000 metres, and was continuously changing direction and height to throw off the ground machine gun fire and air defence cannon. On each balloon I first opened fire at a very short distance and then righted my Albatros and flew close over the balloon and away. Almost all fell to the ground, enveloped by flames, after 15-30 seconds. I attacked no balloon without success, or more than once. Around 1630 hrs all of the captive balloons were down.

'In all, I used 110 phosphorus and 110 K-cartridges, so that I averaged 20 phosphorus and 20 K-cartridges on each balloon. I always carried 460 phosphorus and K-cartridges for each gun, distributed so that the belt of the left gun had four phosphorus and one K, and the belt of the right machine gun had four K and one phosphorus.'

Two of Röth's victims were Balloons Nos 1 and 4 of the Belgian Army. The Belgians subsequently reported seeing three British balloons in flames, but only two of the latter, from KB sections 25-5-2 and 39-8-2, have been positively identified. Röth reported seeing a total of ten parachutes as he flew past his burning victims – apparently all of the observers made it safely to the ground.

Röth managed to down three aeroplanes in July and an SE 5a on 12 August as the war turned against Germany. The following day he

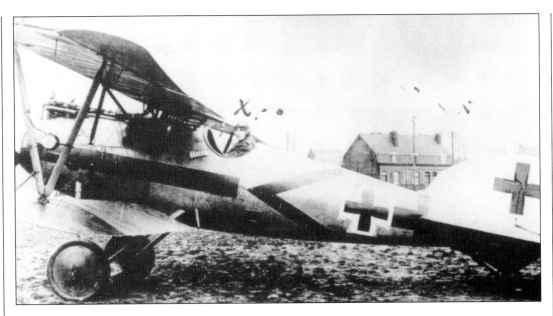

destroyed Belgian balloons Nos 6, 2 and 3 near Lampernisses, then downed a DH 9 on 4 September and an RE 8 on 8 October. Röth scored another 'hat trick' on 10 October between Staden and Ypres over balloons of British KB Section 38-7-2 and the French 25*e* and 91*e* *Compagnies*, but as he shot down a DH 9 of No 108 Sqn over Ledeghem on the 14th, return fire wounded him in the foot. It was his 28th, and final, victory, and the 82nd, and last, for *Jasta* 16b. The rest of the month was mostly spent ground strafing in support of what amounted to a German fighting retreat in the face of a relentless Allied advance.

On 11 November 1918, word reached *Jasta* 16b that the rumoured Armistice had become a reality. 'We flew till noontime', Holtzem recalled. 'Röth, with his leg in a cast, had asked me to show him the frontline in one last flight. The doctor had forbidden him to fly, but he went anyway. He was heartbroken about the ending, and now there was revolution in Germany.'

After risking his life and surviving multifold dangers to become Germany's leading balloon ace with 20 – including a record five in one solo sortie – 'Fritz' Röth would finally succumb to his own depression upon returning to a defeated Germany. Back home in Nuremburg on New Year's Eve, he took his own life. Following his death, he was awarded the Military Order of Max-Josef in much-belated recognition of his first triple victory of 25 January 1918. With that award came knighthood, endowing the factory owner's son with the posthumous title of Friedrich *Ritter* von Röth.

Ltn Martin Demisch of *Jasta* 58 sits in the cockpit of his Albatros D Va at Ennemain in June 1918. Born in Bautzen on 12 November 1896, Demisch (also spelt Dehmisch in some sources) began his scoring with *Jasta* 58 by burning a balloon on 16 June 1918, followed by two more on the 18th. Later flying Fokker D VIIs, he downed three aircraft, as well as more balloons on 6 and 13 September. In a fight with No 40 Sqn on 24 September, Demisch shot down Capt Gilbert J Strange, a seven-victory ace and brother of Col Louis A Strange. Minutes later, Demisch was also brought down near Abancourt by other SE 5as from the unit, probably being credited to Lt J S Smith. The German ace died of his injuries the following day (*Alex Imrie*)

Oblt Röth poses beside the *Jasta* 16b Albatros D Va in which he probably flew his lone balloon strafe of 29 May 1918. Its wings were covered in five-colour camouflage. Note the anemometer-type airspeed indicator above his right shoulder and the auxiliary strut added to stiffen the D Va's unreliable wing structure (*Greg VanWyngarden*)

BALLOON FEVER ON OTHER FRONTS

While the situation on the Western Front often necessitated the elimination of balloons whenever it was not simply providing the specialists a target-rich environment, other fronts tended to favour the loners. The war in Russia alternated dramatically between great, sweeping offensives by one side or the other to long periods of stalemate, during either of which occasion balloons could make an appearance and someone from the other side would sally forth against them.

No Russian ace is known to have included a balloon among his victories, but French ace Sous-Lt Georges Marcel Lachmann, who served in Russia as commander of *Escadrille* N581, destroyed three *Drachen* on 19 September, 3 October and 16 October 1917. An earlier balloon victory, scored over Ham on 15 July 1916 while serving in N57, also figured in his nine-victory total.

German airmen also sortied against the occasional gasbag, and one, Wilhelm Frickart, became the only known balloon ace over Russia. Starting as an observer in Fl. Abt. 24, OfStv Frickart claimed his first victory on 12 April 1917 when he and his pilot, Ltn Leopold Anslinger, downed a Russian Voisin at Pututory – this was Anslinger's fifth of an eventual ten victories. Working with other pilots, Frickart downed another Voisin on 27 April, and then his unit was redesignated Fl. Abt. 242.

In June Frickart enjoyed a startling run of success, destroying Russian balloons on 15, 20 and 24 June. Even more remarkable was an action on 28 June, in which he

French ace Sous-Lt Georges Marcel Lachmann served on the Russia front as commander of *Escadrille* N581 – he is seen here with his SPAD VII. To a previous balloon kill in 1916, he added three *Drachen* over Russia on 19 September, 3 October and 16 October 1917 (*Johan Visser via Jon Guttman*)

Lachmann removes his balaclava after completing a mission in another of his SPAD VIIs. The aircraft features a red-painted cowling and one of several modified grilles that were developed to deal with the SPAD VII's early radiator problems. Note the six empty Le Prieur rocket tubes mounted on the inner set of interplane struts (*SHAA B82.1920*)

The meaning of these numbers chalked on the fuselage side of Lachmann's SPAD VII of N581 remains as enigmatic as his usual red question mark personal marking (*SHAA B76.1806*)

burned a balloon over Folosenkov at 1507 hrs and a second over Telacze at 1542 hrs.

Training to be a pilot, and gaining a leutnant's commission, Frickert returned to action with Fl. Abt. 20, scoring another victory on 17 March 1918 before retraining on fighters and transferring to the Western Front with *Jasta* 64w. On 19 August he moved again, to *Jasta* 65, with whom he twice served as acting commander, downing four more enemy aeroplanes. In addition to the Knight's Cross with Swords of the Hohenzollern House Order, the Iron Cross 1st and 2nd Class, the Silver St Henry Medal and Friedrich-August Medal, 'Willi' Frickart was awarded the Austrian Silver and Bronze Medals for Bravery for his balloon rampage over Russia.

OfStv Wilhelm Frickart downed two Voisins and burned five balloons while serving as an observer over the Russian front. Later earning his pilot's certification and a leutnant's commission, he scored five more victories and survived the war (*Greg VanWyngarden*)

Second to Frickart among Germans over Russia was Hans Martin Pippart. Born on 14 May 1888 in Mannheim, Baden, Pippart had joined Heinrich Noll in 1913 to build monoplanes. When war broke out, he volunteered to fly two-seaters, and on 1 February 1916 he joined newly formed Fl. Abt.(A) 220, which was an artillery-spotting unit assigned to the *Südarmee* in Galicia. While flying Albatros C III 798/16, Vzfw Pippart and his observer, Ltn Schlemmer, attacked Russian balloons on 9 and 10 September, but failed to set them on fire. On 21 November Pippart was commissioned a leutnant and on 18 April 1917 he was attached to a pro-

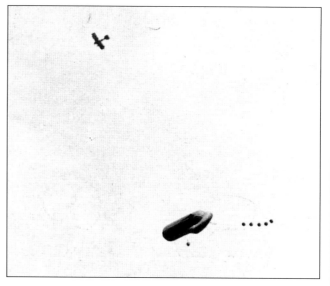

A German two-seater flies past a *Drachen* on the Russian front. Both Wilhelm Frickart and Hans Pippart attacked Russian balloons while flying two-seaters, although Pippart enjoyed more success in single seaters (*Greg VanWyngarden*)

visional *Jagdkommando* (fighter detachment) formed specifically to support Fl. Abt.(A) 220.

Taking to the LFG Roland D II *Haifisch* ('shark') single-seat fighter with growing aggressiveness, Pippart sent a Farman crashing northwest of Siolko on 25 May, then made a succession of attacks on Russian balloons, burning his quarry on 20 and 26 June and 25 August. After downing a Sopwith on 4 October, he destroyed another balloon over Szyrowzy on 23 October.

On 4 December, with the war in Russia winding down (at least for the Germans), Pippart was reassigned to the Western Front, and on the 13th he joined *Jasta* 13, which on 2 February 1918 was combined with *Jastas* 12, 15 and 19 to form *Jagdgeschwader* II. Flying a Fokker Dr I triplane on 21 February, he reopened his account by destroying a balloon of the British 3rd KB Section, 13th Brigade, 5th Balloon Wing (3-13-5), northwest of La Fére. After downing two Breguet 14s, Pippart was given command of *Jasta* 19 on 18 April, and subsequently brought his total up

Pippart's *Haifisch* sits beside
an Albatros C III at Fl. Abt.(A) 220s'
aerodrome, with Roland D IIa (Pfal)
2876/16 of the unit's
Jagdkommando at right
(*Greg VanWyngarden*)

This Pfalz-built Roland D II *Haifisch*
was used by Ltn Hans Martin
Pippart while attached to the
Jagdkommando of Fl. Abt.(A)
220 to destroy four balloons on the
Galician front in 1917. Later flying
with *Jasta* 19 in France, he added
three more balloons to his overall
score of 22 prior to being killed in
action on 11 August 1918 (*Greg
VanWyngarden*)

to 22. His last victory was also his sixth balloon, from 12-16-5 at Brély on
11 August. Later that same day, however, his D VII was shot down in
flames, probably by Breguet 14B2 gunners of Br108 and an escorting
Caudron R 11 from R46. Pippart bailed out at 150 ft – too low for his
parachute to deploy in time to save his life.

Although the Italian front presented fewer opportunies than the West,
occasional balloons had to be disposed of. Italy produced no balloon aces,
and only one could even claim five or more attempts that came close to
success.

Born in Villafranca Lunigiana on 28 July 1895, Sottotenente Flavio
Torello Baracchini had seen previous service as a reconnaissance pilot
when he was assigned to the newly formed *81ᵃ Squadriglia* at Arcade in
April 1916. Flying Nieuports, he became the first fighter pilot to be
awarded the *Medaglia d'Oro al Valore Militare*, and had scored eight
victories by 14 July, when he was transferred to *76ᵃ Squadriglia*. There, he
downed three more enemy aeroplanes, and had his first unsuccessful go at
what he described as 'a small, round enemy balloon' on 7 August.
Baracchini downed an Albatros the next day, but was also wounded in the
left jaw.

In March 1918 Baracchini returned to action with *81ᵃ Squadriglia*,
now equipped with Hanriot HD 1s, and on 3 April he joined in an
inconclusive attack on a balloon at Premaor. Baracchini was credited with

enemy fighters on 2 and 13 May, and on the 18th he and Sergente Raimondo di Loreto punctured, but failed to burn, a *Drachen* at Montello. Four more aeroplanes fell to his guns before he flew another anti-balloon sortie on 18 June, again without confirmation. When he attacked a *Drachen* at Cimadolmo on the 19th, Baracchini came armed with strut-mounted Le Prieur rockets, but three of the four *'turpilles'*, as he called them, failed to ignite.

Sottotenente Michele Allasia poses in a SPAD VII of *77ª Squadriglia* armed with Le Prieur rockets in 1918. Already victor over three aeroplanes with *80ª Squadriglia*, Allasia only logged 37 flying hours and one combat with *77ª* before transferring to *5ª Sezione* SVA and claiming two more successes. He was subsequently killed in a flying accident on 20 July 1918. None of Allasia's five victories were over balloons (*Roberto Gentilli via Jon Guttman*)

In another unsuccessful assault on a balloon at Susegana on the 20th, ground fire struck Baracchini's petrol tank and oil reservoir, and he was fortunate just to return. He finally succeeded on the 21st, with the Austrians noting the loss of *Ballon Kompagnie* 4's *Drachen* to 'a French fighter equipped with rockets', and the successful parachute descent of its observer, Oblt Theodor Tomenko. Baracchini shot down two more enemy aeroplanes on 22 and 25 June, but in the latter combat he suffered an abdominal wound that put him out of the war.

Baracchini's wartime citations credited him with as many as 33 victories, but a post-war review set them officially at 21, for which, in spite of his promotion to captain, his family has remained bitter. Badly burned in an explosion in his chemical laboratory on 29 July 1928, Baracchini died of his injuries in Rome on 18 August that same year.

The most successful Italian ace to tackle balloons was Giovanni Ancillotto. Born in San Donà di Piave, in Venezia province, on 15 November 1896, 'Giannino', or 'Nane', as he was universally known, was an engineering student at the Turin Polytechnic when Italy entered the war. On 4 November 1915 he volunteered for flight training, and on 26 June 1916 Soldato Ancillotto was assigned to *114ª Squadriglia*, later switching to *30ª* on 18 February 1917. His reconnaissance work earned him the *Medaglia d'Argento al Valore Militare*, but on 13 April he left to train on Nieuport fighters.

Sottotenente Giovanni Ancillotto of *77ª Squadriglia* poses beside his Nieuport 11 after scoring his third, final and most spectacular balloon victory on 5 December 1917 – by flying through the burning gasbag! (*Jon Guttman*)

On 14 June Ancillotto joined *80ª Squadriglia*, and on 26 October, while the Italian Army was being routed at Caporetto, he and Sergente Alvaro Leonardi succeeded in driving down a Lohner floatplane. Ancillotto claimed another enemy aircraft that same day, and a third over Doberdò on the 27th. On 3 November he was credited with destroying a German aeroplane, and then, as a semblance of stability was restored at the front, and *80ª* and *77ª Squadriglie* settled in at Marcon aerodrome, near Venice, Ancillotto transferred to the latter squadron.

After escorting a Pomilio two-seater on 15 November, Ancillotto wrote in his combat report;

'I had a combat against three enemy aircraft that attacked a Kite balloon. The combat lasted about ten minutes, but it was not successful because my gun would jam at every bullet. The fighter that flamed the kite balloon carried a red band around its fuselage, and I followed it across the Piave.'

The raiders were from German *Jasta* 31, with Ltn Alwin Thurm burning a balloon at Roncade and Ltn Kosslick destroying another northeast of Treviso. That incident drew Ancillotto's attention to the vast view of the flat plains of the lower Veneto sector that balloons enjoyed, and the consequent artillery fire that the enemy's *Drachen* were able to direct on Italian positions. Those realisations reinforced his resolve to protect his Army's balloons – and to try eliminating the enemy's.

Although *77ª Squadriglia* was primarily equipped with SPAD VIIs, Ancillotto decided to carry out his balloon forays in Nieuport 11 No 2265, which was armed only with interplane strut-mounted Le Prieur rockets. In spite of the obsolescence of his mount, and the unreliability of the only weapons at his disposal, Ancillotto succeeded in sending a *Drachen* down in flames at Fossalta – just across the river from his family villa – on 30 November, which also constituted his fifth victory. On 3 December he made two attacks that failed to destroy his targets, but at least compelled the Austrians to pull them down. On a third raid south of Polo di Piave, however, he succeeded in destroying a *Drachen* in flames.

Ancillotto forced the Austrians to pull down another balloon on 4 December, but it was on the 5th that Giannino entered legend. Going after a *Drachen* at Rustignè, with three SPADs flying escort, he pressed his attack so close that his Nieuport 11 flew across the flaming debris of the exploding gasbag and he returned with large fragments of balloon fabric draped around his damaged scout. That, and his previous exploits, earned Ancillotto a second *Medaglia d'Argento* and, in March 1918, the *Medaglia d'Oro*.

Always game for a new challenge, Ancillotto began to experiment with night patrolling in February 1918, and his efforts bore fruit when he scored Italy's first nocturnal air-to-air victories over Brandenburg C I intruders on 22 and 24 July, for which he received a third *Medaglia d'Argento*. After scoring his tenth victory on 21 August, Ancillotto was assigned to the *Commissariato Generale d'Aeronautica* on 6 September, but he rejoined his old squadron in time to share in the destruction of one more enemy fighter over San Fior with *77ª Squadriglia* commander, Capitano Filippo Serafinia, and two Camels of the No 66 Sqn, on 27 October.

After the war, Ancillotto became a sport flier, flying nonstop from Rome to Warsaw on 11 September 1919, and across the Andes, in Peru, in May 1921. However, on 18 October that same year he was killed in a car crash in Caravaggio.

Three members of the Sopwith Camel squadrons that Britain sent to assist its Italian allies inflicted a particularly stinging toll on the Austro-Hungarian balloon lines in 1917-18. Aggressive dogfighter Capt William George Barker from Dauphin, Manitoba, had already scored his first three victories over Flanders before his unit, No 28 Sqn, RFC, was

Part leader, part loner, Capt William George Barker of No 28 Sqn destroyed nine balloons in Italy, although seven were shared with fellow Canadian ace Lt Harold B Hudson – including five in a single sortie on 12 February 1918. Barker went on to be credited with 50 victories overall and receive the Victoria Cross (*Jon Guttman*)

transferred to Italy. His first success on the Italian Front took the form of an Albatros D V encountered over Pieve de Soligo on 27 November, his wounded victim being Ltn d R Erwin Härtl of German *Jasta* 1, which had likewise gone to Italy to support the Austro-Hungarian offensive both at, and following, Caporetto. Barker's next victims, at 1620 hrs on 3 December, were also German – Ltn Franz von Kerssenbrock of *Jasta* 39, killed in his Albatros northeast of Conegliano, and Ltn M Riegert of *Ballon Kompanie* 10, who was killed in his *Drachen* moments later.

Barker's next success was over a balloon northeast of Pieve de Soligo on 29 December, and on 24 January he destroyed two more east of Conegliano in concert with a fellow Canadian Lt Harold Byron Hudson from Victoria, British Columbia. Bill Barker and 'Steve' Hudson teamed up again for a remarkable series of attacks on the Austro-Hungarian balloon line at Fossamerlo on 12 February, in which they shared in the destruction of five gasbags.

Hudson went on to raise his score to 13, while Barker served in Nos 66 and 139 Sqns in Italy, before returning to Britain to serve as commander of the school of air fighting at Hounslow. In October 1918 he persuaded his superiors to let him return to the Western Front for a 'refresher' in aerial tactics.

After ten days' 'roving commission' in a new Sopwith Snipe attached to No 201 Sqn, on 27 October 1918 Barker went out for a last frontline flight and duly found, and shot down, a Rumpler two-seater over Mormal Woods – and was then promptly jumped by 15 Fokker D VIIs, whose fire wounded him in the thigh. Barker fainted, came to amid the 15 scouts and fought on, claiming three of his antagonists and driving others down, while himself being wounded in the other thigh and an elbow. He finally crash-landed his riddled Snipe in Allied lines and was awarded the Victoria Cross on 30 November, to add to his DSO and Bar, MC and two Bars, *Croix de Guerre* and *Medaglia d'Argento al Valore Militare*.

Tragically killed in a flying accident at Rockliffe, Ontario, on 12 March 1930, Bill Barker was the highest-scoring Canadian balloon ace, but that status seems minor beside his other claims to fame, as the most successful fighter ace over the Italian front (his 43 victories there exceeding Italian Francesco Baracca's 34 and Austrian Godwin Brumowski's 35) and pilot of the single most successful fighter aeroplane of the war, having scored 46 of his 50 victories in the remark-ably long-lived Camel B6313.

The third British balloon ace over Italy was Harry King Goode, who was born in Nuneaton, Warwick-shire in 1895, and who had spent three years in the Royal Engineers before gaining a commission in the RFC in November 1917 and join-ing No 66 Sqn on 27 May 1917. His first victory was over a two-seater on 25 June and his fourth, southeast of Oderzo on 1 August, was also his first balloon kill. He burned another

Pilots of No 28 Sqn smile for the camera in January 1918. They are, from left to right, Lts H B Hudson, G H McLeod and N C Jones. Harold Byron Hudson's 13 accredited victories over Italy included seven *Drachen*, all shared with fellow Canadian Bill Barker. Norman Cyril Jones, from Cheshire in England, was credited with nine enemy aeroplanes destroyed, but eight of them were scored later when serving as a flight commander in No 45 Sqn (*Fleet Air Arm Museum JMB/GSL Collection*)

Aces Hptm Godwin Brumowski (left) and Oblt Frank Linke-Crawford share a joke at *Fliegerkompagnie* 41J's aerodrome at Grossa. Behind them is Brumowski's Oeffag-built Albatros D III 153.52, with what looks like stippled camouflage and skulls on the fuselage sides and upper decking. On the right is Linke-Crawford's falcon-decorated D III 153.16. Brumowski was flying 153.52 when he scored his third balloon victory near Meolo on 13 December 1917 (*Greg VanWyngarden*)

Overpainted red in emulation of Manfred von Richthofen, and also adorned with a skull, Albatros D III 153.52 was written off after Godwin Brumowski narrowly escaped the attentions of eight Camels on 4 February 1918, crash-landing at *Flik* 41J's new airfield at Passarella (*Greg VanWyngarden*)

over Ozerzo on 16 October for his tenth overall success, and on the 22nd he and Capt H Hindle-James teamed up to eliminate a balloon southwest of Vazzolo. Goode's final victories were all over Austrian *Drachen* – one on the 27th, two on the 28th and one on 29 October. After despatching the latter for his 15th, and final, victory, Goode shot up the aerodrome at South Gioncomo, claiming to have destroyed three aeroplanes on the ground.

Awarded the DSO and DFC for his wartime achievements, Goode remained in the RAF until his retirement as a group captain in December 1941. Goode carried on as a civilian employee with the Accident Branch of the RAF, but he was killed when the Consolidated Liberator of No 120 Sqn on which he was a passenger crashed on 21 August 1941.

Only two Austro-Hungarian aces were credited with five or more balloons. As was the case with the Americans, they included the leading ace of the *Kaiserliche und Königliche Luftfahrtruppen* (Imperial and Royal Air Troops).

Born into a military family in Wadowice, Galicia, on 26 July 1889, Godwin Brumowski attended the Technical Military Academy at Mödling, before being commissioned a leutnant in the field artillery in 1910. In July 1915 he was assigned as an observer to *Fliegerkompagnie* (*Flik*) 1 on the Russian front, and on 12 April 1916 Brumowski was in the back seat of a Knoller-Albatros B I flown by *Flik* 1's commander, Hptm Otto Jindra, when the latter led six other aeroplanes in a bombing attack on a Russian military review in Chotin – with Tsar Nicholas II and General Aleksei Brusilov in attendance. To add further injury to insult, Jindra and Brumowski downed two of the seven Morane-Saulnier Parasols that rose to challenge the raiders.

Later earning his pilot's certificate in July 1916, Brumowski raised his score to five and was then given command of *Flik* 41J – the *KuK Luftfahrtruppen*'s first pure fighter

77

unit – in February 1917. Before taking charge, however, Brumowski visited the Western Front, where he flew missions with German *Jasta* 24 in order to get a few useful pointers on aerial tactics and strategy from *Jasta* 11's leader, Manfred *Freiherr* von Richthofen.

Returning to *Flik* 41J in April 1917, Brumowski moulded the unit into an Austrian version of Richthofen's 'Flying Circus', leading several aces and steadily adding to his own score. His 22nd victory on 9 October 1917 was also his first balloon, which collapsed in flames near the Isola Morosina, although its observer (Tenente Guido Venditelli of *20ª Sezione*) parachuted to safety. This victory was also his first success in Oeffag-built Albatros D III 153.45, which was the first of several that Hptm Brumowski, betraying an obvious Richthofen influence, painted red overall, with the addition of black-enshrouded white skulls on the fuselage sides and upper decking.

After sharing in the destruction of two Macchi L-3 flying boats on 5 November, Brumowski and Stfw Karoly Kaszala burned a balloon along the Piave River estuary on the 17th, the gasbag's observer again successfully bailing out. In another team-up on 13 December, Brumowski, Kaszala and Oblt Frank Linke-Crawford destroyed a balloon in flames near Meolo.

Brumowski bagged his last two gasbags during the pivotal Battle of the Piave. On 16 June 1918 he destroyed one at Spresiano, probably of *3º Gruppo*, from which Capitano V Morpurgo bailed out safely. Amid a welter of air activity on the 19th, he burned a balloon of *11ª Sezione*, carrying Tenente M Zanini, near Passarella, shared in the destruction of a two-seater south of Candelu with Oblt Rupert Terk, commander of *Flik* 63J, and finished the day with an Ansaldo SVA 5. He returned to his aerodrome with 37 bullet holes in his Albatros D III, 153.209. These successes brought Brumowski's total up to 35.

His many decorations included the Order of the Iron Crown, 3rd Class with War Decoration, the Knight's Cross of the Order of Leopold with War Decoration and Swords and the Gold Bravery Medal for Officers, but oddly it did not include Austria-Hungary's highest honour, the Knight's Cross of the Military Order of Maria Theresa. The defeat and dissolution of the Austro-Hungarian Empire was particularly traumatic to Brumowski. Weary of running the family estate after the war, in 1930 he returned to aviation as a flight instructor at Aspern, but on 3 June 1936 he was mortally injured when his aeroplane crashed at Schiphol Airport, in the Netherlands.

Austria's other balloon ace was Eugen Bönsch, who was born of Sudeten German parents in Gross-Aupa, near Trautenau in northern Bohemia (now the Czech Republic), on 1 May 1897. After studying mechanics and machine manufacturing at the State Trade School, he volunteered for the Army and eventually transferred to the *KuK Luftfahrtruppen*. Bönsch initially served as a mechanical engineer with *Fliegerersatzkompagnie* 6, but in 1917 he requested flight training and was assigned to *Flik* 51J in August of that year.

His first victory (an Italian Nieuport) was shared with three other pilots on 1 September. On the 28th, he and Ltn Sandor Tahy fought their way through stiff resistance, including an Italian Nieuport and a SPAD VII, to attack a balloon north of Plava. Coming in at a height of 700 metres,

Proudly wearing his medals, and standing second from right in the second row, Eugen Bönsch is seen with other *Flik* 51J personnel at Ghirano in the summer of 1918

Conspicuous by their absence in this photograph of Ltn Rudolf von Eschwege, taken on the Macedonian front, is his flying badge or his Iron Cross 1st Class (*Walter A Musciano via Jon Guttman*)

Bönch's Oeffag-Albatros 153.35 suffered damage from ground fire, but his repeated passes finally caused the gasbag to catch fire and its observer, Tenente Paolo Calisse, bailed out. For his tenacious courage, Bönsch received the Gold Medal for Bravery – the highest award for a noncommissioned officer. He shared in the destruction of a Nieuport the following day with Tahy and Oblt Georg Kenzian von Kenzianhausen.

On 3 December Bönsch and Fw István Fejes disposed of another balloon, but he was reminded of what made these sorties so dangerous exactly a month later when AA fire brought him down south of Motta in Albatros D III 135.31. Returning to action in the new year, he shared in bringing down Camels on 21 February and 16 March 1918.

April saw Bönsch attack a variety of Italian ground targets, including a balloon destroyed southwest of San Biaggio on the 3rd. After he and Ltn Franz Rudorffer downed a SAML 2 on the 17th, Bönsch attacked a balloon on 3 May – although the result could not be confirmed, he received a second Gold Medal. He had better luck on 16 June amid the Battle of the Piave, although it was only on his third pass, amid intensifying AA fire at a height of just 50 metres, that his target finally exploded in flames near Breda di Piave. The observer, Sottotenente Umberto Fraticelli of *7ª Sezione*, had already parachuted clear.

Bönsch downed a photoreconnaissance aeroplane on 20 June, and although the Battle of the Piave ended in Allied victory, Bönsch's achievements earned him a third Gold Medal for Bravery. This was an honour he shared with just five other NCOs during the war.

As fortune turned against Austria-Hungary, at 2047 hrs on 8 August Bönsch attacked a Type AP balloon of *2ª Sezione Aerostatica Autocampale* near Vascon-Carbonera, from which the section commander, Capitano Salvatore Salis, and Sottotenente Guido Luria bailed out before their gasbag exploded. On 5 October Bönsch burned his fifth balloon west of Ponti di Piave, and on the 27th – the third day of the Battle of Vittorio Veneto – he brought down an RE 8 of No 34 Sqn, RAF, along with another Camel in concert with Rudorffer. The next day Bönsch downed a Hanriot HD 1, killing Tenente Carlo Pasquinelli of *78ª Squadriglia*. On the 29th he claimed another Hanriot over Papadopoli Island for his 16th victory, before being shot down in flames. Bönsch used his parachute – now employed in Austro-Hungarian aeroplanes as well as balloons – to alight safely west of the Piave, then made his way across the river to rejoin his unit.

The Battle of Vittorio Veneto ended on 3 November, and with it, for all intents and purposes, the Hapsburg Dual Monarchy.

After the war, Bönsch owned an inn in the northern Bohemian mountains, and during World War 2 he served in the *Luftwaffe*, rising to

A squadronmate in one of Fl. Abt. 30's normal complement of two-seaters took this photograph of Ltn Rudolf von Eschwege in his Albatros D III in the spring of 1917. The only distinguishing markings visible are the wing crosses, which are applied farther inboard than usual, in typical Austro-Hungarian style (*Walter A Musciano via Jon Guttman*)

A British anti-aircraft gun mounted on an automobile waits in a camouflaged position on the Balkan front. When conventional weapons failed to end von Eschwege's balloon-busting spree, the British resorted to a ruse that left a sour taste in some of their own mouths (*Jon Guttman*)

the rank of hauptmann in command of the Oschatz airbase in Saxony. After the war Eugen Bönsch lived in his brother's hotel in Ehrwald, west of Innsbruck, in the Tyrol, and never spoke of his wartime exploits even to members of his family, until his death on 24 July 1951.

Italian Giovanni Ancillotto was not the only ace on a lesser-known front who did not have to shoot down five balloons for his name to be associated with them. Born in Bad Homburg von de Hohe on 25 February 1895, Rudolph von Eschwege had served in the 3rd Mounted *Jäger* Regiment before transferring to the *Luftstreitskräfte* in 1915.

After flying reconnaissance missions over the Western Front with Fl. Abt. 36, in the autumn of 1916 he was transferred to the Macedonian Front and served with Fl. Abt. 66 and 30. There, German, Bulgarian and Turkish air detachments had to face French and Franco-Serbian *escadrilles* and squadrons of the British RFC and RNAS that sometimes outnumbered them 10-to-1. Flying Fokker Eindecker and later biplane fighters, 'Rudi' von Eschwege accepted that challenge with remarkable élan, scoring his first official victory over a Nieuport 12 of 2 Wing, RNAS, on 19 November 1916. In the following year Eschwege acquired an Albatros D III and scored steadily, earning him a reputation for relentless courage combined with chivalry and such sobriquets as 'Eagle of the Aegean' and 'Richthofen of the Balkans'.

After bringing down a BE 12 of No 17 Sqn for his 16th victory on 3 October 1917, Eschwege turned his attention to a British gasbag of the 17th Kite Balloon Section that appeared every morning over Orljak, west of the Struma River, to direct artillery fire. Loading his guns with incendiary ammunition on the morning of 28 October, he circled through the mountains north of Seres before approaching his target with the sun behind him. The observer took to his parachute, and Eschwege had to make four passes at the balloon in order to set it alight. He then just barely escaped from a vengeful posse of Allied fighters.

In spite of the unexpected difficulties and dangers involved – or perhaps because of them – Eschwege became fascinated with 'roasting sausages', and on 9 November he attacked another over Kopiva, killing the observer but failing to set the balloon on fire before his guns jammed. On the 15th, however, he succeeded in destroying a replacement gasbag of the 17th KB Section over Orljak.

When next he sortied on the 19th, Eschwege encountered a Sopwith 1^1/$_2$ Strutter of No 17 Sqn, which he shot down near Kalendra, west of Seres. As he bore in on the balloon that the RFC aircraft had been covering, the British winched it to the ground. The frustrated German

then turned on four other Allied aeroplanes in the gasbag's vicinity, but they fled.

Eschwege was up at dawn on 21 November for another strike at the 17th KB Section's latest 'eye in the sky' over Orljak. A Bulgarian officer in charge of a mountain observation post north of Seres, spotting the balloon through his binoculars that morning, noted that it was higher than usual – 2500 ft, rather than the usual 500 to 1000 ft – and that there were no aeroplanes patrolling nearby. When he saw Eschwege's Albatros approaching the gasbag, he alerted his comrades to watch the show, but also noticed a curious lack of defensive AA fire around the balloon. Moments later, as Eschwege pulled up over his now-burning target, a large puff of smoke enveloped his Albatros, then it banked sharply and dived earthward.

RFC medics and technicians examine the remains of von Eschwege and his Albatros D III after their explosive-rigged balloon brought him down on 21 November 1917 (*IWM via Walter A Musciano*)

A few days later, a British aeroplane flew over Fl. Abt. 30's airfield at Drama and dropped a message. 'To the Bulgarian-German Flying Corps in Drama. The officers of the Royal Flying Corps regret to announce that Ltn von Eschwege was killed while attacking the captive balloon. His personal belongings will be dropped over the lines some time during the next few days'. True to their word, they airdropped his effects, along with photographs of his burial with full military honours.

Although it was credited as his 20th victory, Eschwege had in fact been the victim of his quarry. The British, frustrated and embarrassed by the havoc that the lone German ace was causing over their sector, and taking note of his recent fixation with balloons, had sent up a repaired, but operationally unserviceable, gasbag manned by a straw dummy covered with an old uniform and sat in the observer's basket – along with 500 lbs of explosives. As Eschwege closed in, the British detonated the device from the ground. Pleased though it was to be rid of the aerial menace, the RFC's official account betrayed a tinge of guilt. 'He came to his end as a

This photograph of von Eschwege's funeral, with six British officers carrying his coffin to burial with honours, was probably the one dropped at his aerodrome at Drama to inform his unit of his death. (*Ministry of Defence courtesy Henry Tremont*)

result of a legitimate ruse of war, but there was no rejoicing among the pilots of the squadrons which had suffered from his activities. They would had preferred that he had gone down in fair combat'.

Unsporting or not, there would be at least one further recorded attempt to eliminate a balloon specialist over the Western Front using a basket full of explosives. As will be seen, however, the would-be victim would cause the scheme to backfire – literally.

THE GREATEST OF THEM ALL

The leading balloon buster of all time also happens to be the highest-scoring – and, in utter defiance of the odds, longest-lived – of the five Belgian aces of World War 1. Born in Watermaal-Boosvoorde, near Brussels, on 6 July 1892, Willy Omer François Jean Coppens spent the pre-war years indulging in such early passions as designing and building wheeled, sail-propelled land yachts. He built seven such vehicles between 1907 and 1913. In 1910, Coppens saw his first aeroplane, and instantly yearned to fly, but his artist father threatened to throw him out of the house if he did. Willy settled for building and flying kites and model aeroplanes until 1912, when he was conscripted into military service and joined the 2nd Grenadier Regiment.

When war broke out in August 1914, the Belgian Army was swiftly driven back into France, leaving Coppens' family in Brussels, and him, with a lifeling hatred of the German invaders. Transferring to the Belgian Motor Machine Gun Corps, he also acquired a dislike for the trenches, and on 6 September 1915 he signed up for flight training at Beaumarais. The ill-equipped Belgian school was incapable of providing him with the training, so Coppens went on eight weeks' leave and took private lessons in England to obtain Royal Aero Club Certificate No 2140 on 9 December, then completed his training at the Farman School at Etampes, in France.

Coppens' first combat assignment, in the winter of 1917, was with *6ème Escadrille d'Observation*, flying BE 2cs from Houthem aerodrome. Promoted to sergent 1ére class on 8 April, he transferred to *4ème Escadrille* later that month, this unit being equipped with obsolescent Farman pushers. On 1 May he received a Sopwith 1¹/₂ Strutter, and later that same day he experienced his first combat. Coppens' aeroplane had not yet had its front machine gun installed, but he did his best to evade his four attackers while his observer, Capitaine R Declercq, fended them off with his Lewis gun. The crew returned with 32 bullet holes in the aeroplane.

On 7 July Coppens and Declercq engaged a German two-seater and sent it diving away near Middlekerke. One week later the aggressive young pilot finally got what he wanted – a transfer to fly single-seat fighters with *1ére Escadrille de*

Willy Coppens is seen in the cockpit of his *1ére Escadrille, Aviation Militaire Belge,* Nieuport 16, the fighter featuring his blue cocotte, or paper horse, personal marking. This also appeared on one of his later Hanriot HD 1s until his redesignated unit, *9ème Escadrille,* adopted the thistle as its emblem. The cocotte later reappeared as the *11ème Escadrille* insignia (*Willy Coppens album via Jon Guttman*)

Chasse, based at Les Moëres. There, Coppens found role models in the unit's myopic commander, Capitaine Fernand Jacquet, who had become Belgium's first ace by engaging German aircraft at point-blank range in a Farman F 40 two-seat pusher. Fellow ace Sgt Jan Olieslagers, who was a bicycle racing champion and pre-war aviator, and who would eventually be credited with six victories even though he never claimed any, was also on the squadron. Finally, Coppens' flight leader, Lt André De Meulemeester, was also a sharp-eyed hunter who would survive the war with 11 victories.

1ére Escadrille was equipped with Nieuport 17s, but Coppens was assigned what was probably the last Nieuport 16 left on the Western Front! Although still inexperienced in the tricky machine, on 21 July 1917 he attacked a German two-seater and was shot-up for his trouble. Coppens was promoted to adjutant on 19 August, and several weeks later his squadron received the first of a batch of Hanriot HD 1s that the *Aviation Militaire Belge* had acquired because the French, sold on SPADs, did not want them.

De Meulemeester rejected the new fighter out of hand, as did everyone else save Coppens, whose subsequent glowing reports of its flight characteristics convinced the squadron to accept it! He later recalled;

'But the HD 1 had a great defect – only one machine gun, because De Meulemeester, our ace in 1917, decided it better to climb 800 ft higher. With two it climbed only just over 20,000 ft.

'The Hanriot HD 1 aeroplanes of my squadron had all of their vertical surfaces (save for the rudder, painted red, yellow and black) and horizontal upper surfaces camouflaged with French camouflage colours, The horizontal undersurfaces were painted an aluminium colour. The colours of the flights were only on the cowling, but the green and white of Olieslagers' flight were changed after a few days and painted to show equilateral triangles. The vertical stabiliser of the tail was camouflaged, and each pilot had his colours on the upper side of the horizontal empennage. Olieslagers had long white and green triangles.

'My Hanriot had a cocotte for short time, as I had to paint the thistle of the squadron when that badge was decided (during one of my leaves) in spite of my idea that a thistle never attacked! I had a blue and white fan.'

The latter, along with a white cowling, appeared on Coppens' HD 1s Nos '17' and '24'.

On 10 September 1917 a new SPAD XIII fighter landed at Les Moëres with engine trouble, and from its cockpit emerged a frustrated Capitaine Georges Guynemer, then France's ace of aces with 53 victories. 'Having been forced to land at an unknown field', Coppens recalled, 'Guynemer appeared to be a little nervous, and not very talkative. He was not distant nor timid, but seemed a bit uneasy because of our intense curiosity. He had shaken hands with the first of us to come to him, without knowing who we were. Then he paid attention to our mechanics at work, putting his Hispano in order. We would have liked, all of us, to ask him questions.

'My old friend Jacques Ledure, a pilot who was very clever with motors, watched and gave good advice. He exchanged ideas with Guynemer and, to please me, succeeded in having the ace sign my silver cigarette case. When his motor was in order, and tested, Guynemer flew off, straight to St Pol. None of us ever saw him again.'

Adjutant Coppens stands before Hanriot HD 1 Nº 17, in which he flew behind enemy lines to 'look up' his parents in German-occupied Brussels on 18 February 1918. The royal blue fan personal marking on the white tailplane also appeared on Coppens' HD 1 Nº 24 (*Walter Pieters*)

Guynemer was killed in action the very next day, and Coppens had new cause for revenge.

Although confirmed successes eluded the Belgian over the following months, he gained his first measure of notoriety by venturing 200 kilometres into German territory so as to fly over Brussels on 18 February 1918. He gave his own account of this seemingly suicidal gesture:

'With full tanks, I took off at 0835 hrs. Half-an-hour later, at 0905 hrs, I was at a height of 18,000 ft above Dixmuide. The enemy anti-aircraft defense was fully busy chasing two French SPADs, and I think that it was thanks to those circumstances that they did not aim at me, and that I passed unnoticed.'

At 0952 hrs Coppens arrived over the Belgian capital for the first time since the Germans had overrun it three-and-a-half years earlier. Diving from 3000 ft, he made his way to the Rue des Champs Elysées, facing the Parc Solvay, where his parents lived.

'The Hanriot made it possible to turn inside a very short radius, and in this way I made a tour of the house five times, so low that I nearly touched the tops of the trees', he continued. 'On the second tour, I saw, and recognised my father, who was looking out of one of the upper windows. I was so near that I could distinguish details of his clothing – he was wearing a brown necktie, the same colour as his suit. He made wild movements of his arm, and his emotion must have come up to mind. I also saw my mother, on the first floor, behind a window, the reflection of which prevented me from seeing exactly, but it must have been she. She had been the first to hear the aeroplane, and to feel sure that it was me.

'At the Place Saints-Croix, quite near, there was incredible animation, which I noticed on each tour while passing the house. An hour later the whole city knew my name, and there were even a lot of people who, later on, said that they recognised me! At 1045 hrs I landed on Les Moëres airfield. My folly was well acknowledged.'

This, and past brushes with death, convinced Coppens that he was too lucky to let fear affect his personal war against the Germans, yet his efforts to do damage to them remained frustratingly elusive. Then, on 17 March 1918, the enemy seized two key guard posts at Riegersvliet from elements of the Belgian Cavalry Division. The horsemen felt it a matter of honour to recover both posts, but their prospects were handicapped by the presence of a German balloon monitoring the sector from Bovekerke.

Sgt-Maj Charles de Montigny and Coppens volunteered to bring the *Drachen* down, and in spite of having no incendiary ammunition, they at least succeeded in puncturing the gasbag and forcing its observer to bail out. They then repeated their performance on a second, replacement *Drachen*, depriving the Germans of their services just long enough for the Belgian cavalry to retake the two posts.

From then on, whenever the Belgians needed a volunteer to deal with an enemy balloon, Coppens accepted the job. 'I had started attacking the *Drachen* by sense of duty', he explained. 'I went on by pride'.

He finally scored his first confirmed victory on 25 April – a Rumpler two-seater that he and Capitaine Walter Gallez sent crashing near St Joris. Soon afterward, Coppens managed to wangle an allotment of 20 incendiary rounds a month from his superiors, four of which he installed in his ammunition belt for each mission. To make them count, he made it his inviolable policy to never fire at ranges greater than 150 yards. He first tested that tactic on 8 May, when he came so close to a *Drachen* over Zarren that he almost struck it, but succeeded in setting it afire. Returning to his aerodrome to reload with four more incendiaries, Coppens found another balloon over the Houthulst Forest, and coming down on it from above, burned it as well. For the day's double success he was congratulated by King Albert I and awarded the *Croix de Guerre* and *Ordre de la Couronne*.

During a foray on 15 May, Coppens learned to his dismay that the morning dew had literally dampened the likelihood of his setting a *Drachen* alight. He nevertheless made three attacks through heavy AA fire in an effort to destroy another balloon over Houthulst, but without result. Blipping his rotary engine to low speed and coming in at the *Drachen*'s level, he tried once more, firing his last 30 rounds into it. Although the balloon still did not burn, his long burst apparently severed its cables, for just as he began climbing above it, it suddenly shot upward, colliding with his HD 1. Coppens turned off his engine, lest his propeller foul in the fabric, and waited in terrified suspense as his Hanriot slid and tumbled along the sagging gasbag until it finally fell over the side. He pointed the nose of his scout earthward to build up speed, then switched on the engine and, when it roared back to life, pulled up and away while the perforated balloon descended to earth and exploded.

To the scepticism expressed by Olieslagers and De Meulemeester when told of his claim, Coppens pointed to scars left on his propeller blades by the cables, and traces of balloon fabric on his wing and undercarriage.

A more auspicious day for Coppens came four days later when he 'roasted another sausage' over Houthulst for his ace-making fifth victory. Soon after that, he received a gift from the French – an 11 mm Vickers machine gun with incendiary ammunition, specially built for balloon-busting. Delighted, he installed it on his Hanriot and used it to despatch *Drachen* on 5, 9, and 10 June.

Disaster struck *9ème Escadrille* on the night of 13 June, when a German night bombing raid caused a fire in its hangar, destroying or damaging all of the unit's Hanriots, including Coppens' HD 1s '17' and '24'. He got a replacement on the 18th in the form of Hanriot '6', but later wrote, 'It

Four of Belgium's five aces can be seen in this photograph of Sous-Lt Coppens' Hanriot HD 1 N° 24 after he had scored his fifth victory on 19 May 1918. Lt Jan Olieslagers, who had scored his sixth victory the same day, is congratulating Coppens at right, with Adjutant André De Meulemeester flanking him. Second from left is Capitaine Fernand Jacquet (*Walter Pieters*)

had been re-covered at Beaumarais (Calais), where they had camouflaged it in an asinine fashion. It resembled one of those varnished wooden snakes you saw in toyshops. At the first opportunity, I had my machine painted blue all over'.

De Meulemeester had previously flown 'No 6', fitted with twin 0.303-in Vickers machine guns, only to reject the arrangement. Coppens later flew it with the 11 mm machine gun.

He destroyed another balloon over Ploegsteert and a Hannover CL III over Warneton on 24 June, but after he landed, De Meulemeester found him trembling in the cockpit. When his flight leader asked if he was hit, Coppens whispered, 'I just killed a brave man, and I killed him in the worst way I could. The balloon observer didn't jump – he kept firing at me with a little handgun. The burning balloon just swallowed him up'.

Although that image would haunt Coppens for the rest of his life, it did not prevent him from accepting a promotion to sous-lieutenant, or from finishing June with a 'hat trick' on the 30th – a balloon over Boverkerke at 0630 hrs, another at Gheluvelt at 0830 hrs and a third over Passchendaele four minutes later.

Coppens' royal blue Hanriot was becoming all too familiar a sight to the Germans, who referred to him as *'der blaue Teufel'*. 'The result of my frequent attacks was that the balloons did not go so high anymore (900 metres instead of 1200) or come so near to our lines (eight to twelve kilometres, instead of six)', he remarked. The Germans also doubled and tripled the number of gun batteries around their balloon nests.

After some leave to be made a *Chevalier de l'Ordre de Léopold*, Coppens resumed his scoring on France's Bastille Day, followed by more balloons on the 16th, 19th and 20th, and another 'hat trick' over Gheluwe, Wervicq and Comines between 0730 and 0734 hrs on the 22nd, for which the British in that sector awarded him the Military Cross.

Coppens burned a *Drachen* at Ruyterhoek on 24 July, but while attacking another over Reutel at 0750 hrs on 3 August, his aeroplane was shaken by an explosion, although he managed to recover control. After he returned, the Belgians learned from an enemy prisoner that the Germans had sent that last balloon up packed with explosives to blast the 'Blue Devil' back to hell, just as the British had done to Rudolf von Eschwege in 1917. 'Unfortunately – for the Germans – I had dived out of the sky before the final arrangements had been completed', Coppens wrote, 'and had sent the "sausage" down, nicely roasted, with its charge of explosive, into the center of the assembled spectators!'

Coppens scored another triple on 10 August, and on the 22nd he was given command of a three-aeroplane flight. Two days later he burned two more balloons, followed by more on 3 and 4 September. On the 7th he donned his dress uniform to receive the Belgian *Légion d'Honneur* from King Albert and the *Croix de Guerre* from French Prime Minister Georges Clemenceau, who, much to the ace's amusement, while bending over to pin the award on the diminutive Belgian, bumped his head on Coppens' helmet! He subsequently added the French *Légion d'Honneur*, the British DSO, the Serbian Order of the White Eagle, and decorations from Portugal, Italy and Poland to his international collection.

In mid-September Coppens received two more HD 1s, Nos '23' and '45'. 'No 23', he stated, 'had an ugly and bad camouflage painted in Calais. I had it for a second aeroplane, and painted it in a beautiful royal blue, not dark, not pale. Hanriot very generously gave me a larger elevator off an HD 2, which I put on my blue HD 1 – it rolled much better, allowing me to turn immediately when I was attacked, make a half-roll and pass under my attacker, who did not know where I had passed, until he heard me firing at him'.

Coppens burned two *Drachen* over Leffinghe on 27 September and another two days later, although while returning from the latter raid he

Sous-Lt Coppens poses in the cockpit of one of his camouflaged HD 1s, showing details of the aircraft's cabane strut arrangement and modest armament (*IWM Q79166 via Jon Guttman*)

came under fire from a nervous RE 8 crew, for which he lodged a protest with the RAF. On 2 October he and Sgt Étienne Hage drove a German two-seater down out of control, but it went unconfirmed. Returning to his forte, Coppens burned a *Drachen* on the 3rd and two more on the 5th, raising his tally to 35.

The Allies were by then advancing on all fronts, and with their offensive about to resume on 14 October, Coppens set out at 0540 hrs with Hage to eliminate the *Drachen* at Tourhout. Along the way Coppens spotted another gasbag 1800 feet above Praatbos, near Dixmuide and, diving and expending only four rounds, caused it to explode at 0600 hrs.

Moving on to Tourhout, the Belgians found their quarry at 2400 ft, but as Coppens approached to within 500 metres, he was suddenly hit by a hollow machine gun round that smashed the tibia of his left leg and severed the artery. The sudden agonised spasm caused his right leg to kick the rudder bar, throwing his aeroplane into a spin, with his machine gun still spraying the air. 'The first of these bullets at least hit the balloon, which burst into flames', Coppens recalled, 'but it was a thing I did not know at the time, and I did not claim a victory'.

Though throbbing with pain and rapidly bleeding to death, Coppens was determined not to fall into German hands, dead or alive. Using his right leg to work the rudder bar, he came out of his spin and, in spite of a bullet hole in the inlet pipe of his engine, flew the five to six miles to Allied lines in three nerve-wracking minutes. 'I wanted air, ice-cold air, to bathe my face and keep me from fainting', he recalled, for which reason he threw off his goggles and scarf, although he stuffed his fur-lined flying helmet in his coat. When the sound of gunfire ceased, he said, 'I chose a small field by the side of the road, on which a fair amount of traffic told me that I should obtain help. The field, all too small, was hemmed in with hedges, and I had to put my machine down rather heavily in order to arrest its progress. My undercarriage, which had been badly weakened by the machine gun fire, collapsed on contact with the ground'.

Stretcher-bearers arrived and rushed Coppens to hospital at La Panne, where his left leg had to be amputated. Hage, he later learned, had subsequently found and destroyed a third balloon over Roulers, before he too was wounded in the arm. King Albert visited Coppens the next day, and invested him with the rosette of an *Officier de l'Ordre de Léopold*.

After the Armistice and the liberation of his country, Coppens was made Baron d'Houthulst and persuaded to stay in the Army by the King himself. When he left the service in 1940, however, he had only attained the rank of major, having spent much of his time as a military attaché in Italy, Switzerland, France and Britain. During World War 2 he resided in Switzerland, organising resistance work and marrying.

In the late 1960s he moved back to Belgium and lived his last five years with Jan Olieslagers' only daughter. Coppens' memoir, *Jours Envoles*, was translated into English in 1932 as *Days on the Wing*, and he also wrote a biography of Olieslagers and was working on one for Italian ace Fulco Ruffo di Calabria when he died on 21 December 1986. Sudden and saddening though his death was, Coppens had not only been Belgium's ace of aces, and the leading balloon-buster of all time, but one of the longest-lived survivors of an extremely high-risk speciality.

This commemorative medal was struck in honour of Willy Coppens shortly after World War 1 (*Willy Coppens album via Jon Guttman*)

An estimated 500 kite balloons were employed by each side over the Western Front, and they came to symbolise the trench warfare that made them such a fixture. When the Armistice went into effect on 11 November 1918, a British communiqué announced it by declaring, 'All along the Front, the balloons are down'.

Kite balloons occasionally saw further use in later years – on 31 May 1943, for example, the Soviet Union's female ace of aces, Lydia V Litvyak, crossed the lines and circled back to surprise a German balloon nest from behind and destroy the observation gasbag. Such incidents, however, were the exception to the rule during World War 2, in which more advanced aeroplanes had become the predominant vehicle for gathering aerial intelligence, and tethered lighter-than-air craft were put to other work, most notably as barrage balloons. World War 1 had marked the apogee of the observation balloon, both as a target of strategic importance and as a challenge to the airmen who tried to eliminate it. Coppens and his colleagues represented a unique breed from a unique time. Aviation history is unlikely to see their like again.

'Puppchen' – a gasbag operated by *Ballonzug* 112 at Côte Lorraine in May 1918, illustrating that the early type *Drachen* were still in some use that late in the war. Coppens destroyed a handful of these during his 'sausage roasting' rampage over the Western Front in 1918 (*Tom Darcey Collection via Greg VanWyngarden*)

APPENDICES

Balloon Aces' Scores

Pilot	Nationality	Total Balloons Destroyed	Balloons Destroyed In One Day	Total score
Willy Coppens, Baron d'Houthulst	Belgian	35	3	37
Jean Pierre Bourjade	French	27	3	27
Michel Coiffard	French	24	3	34
Maurice Boyau	French	21	2	35
Fritz Röth	German	20	5	28
Jacques Ehrlich	French	18	3	19
Heinrich Gontermann	German	17	4	39
Anthony W Beauchamp-Proctor	South African	16	2	54
Frank Luke	American	14	3	18
Karl Schlegel	German	14	2	22
Oskar Hennrich	German	13	3	20
Claude Haegelen	French	12	2	22
Marius Ambrogi	French	11	2	14
Fritz Friedrichs	German	11	2	21
Henry W Woollett	English	11	3	35
Tom Falcon Hazell	Irish	10	2	43
Friedrich Höhn	German	10	2	21
Max Näther	German	10	-	26
William G Barker	Canadian	9	5*	50
Louis Bennett Jr	American	9	3	12
Henri Condemine	French	9	3	9
Hans von Freden	German	9	2	20
Sidney W Highwood	English	9	3	16
Jean André Pezon	French	9	-	10
Armand Pinsard	French	9	-	27
Erich Thomas	German	9	2	10
Paul Barbreau	French	8	2	8
Josef Jacobs	German	8	2	41
Max Kuhn	German	8	2	12
Charles Macé	French	8	2	12
Ernest Manoury	French	8	2	11
Friedrich Noltenius	German	8	-	21
Friedrich Pütter	German	8	2	25
Otto Schmidt	German	8	-	20
Maurice Bizot	French	7	-	10

Pilot	Nationality	Total Balloons Destroyed	Balloons Destroyed In One Day	Total score
Oskar *Freiherr* von Boenigk	German	7	-	25
Harold B Hudson	Canadian	7	5*	13
Hans Nülle	German	7	4	1
Charles Nungesser	French	7	4	43
Hans Pippart	German	7	-	22
Paul Santelli	French	7	-	7
Julius Buckler	German	6	2	36
Siegfried Büttner	German	6	2	13
Antoine Laplasse	French	6	3	8
Donald R MacLaren	Canadian	6	-	54
Georg Meyer	German	6	-	24
Marcel Bloch	French	5	-	5
Eugen Bönsch	Austrian	5	-	16
Fernand Bonneton	French	5	-	9
Godwin Brumowski	Austrian	5	-	35
William C Campbell	Scottish	5	2	23
Pierre Cardon	French	5	2	5
Sydney Carlin	English	5	-	10
Arthur H Cobby	Australian	5	-	29
Martin Dehmisch	German	5	2	10
Pierre Ducornet	French	5	2	7
Wilhelm Frickart	German	5	2	12
Harry K Goode	English	5	2	15
Louis Gros	French	5	-	9
François Guerrier	French	5	2	5
Heinrich Haase	German	5	-	6
Lansing C Holden	American	5	-	7
Jacques Leps	French	5	-	12
Richard B Munday	Australian	5	-	9
Maurice Nogues	French	5	2	13
Edward Vernon Rickenbacker	American	5	-	26
George R Riley	English	5	3	13
Gilbert Sardier	French	5	2	15
William E Shields	Canadian	5	2	24
Walter A Southey	South African	5	2	20
Yvon Paul Robert Waddington	French	5	-	12
Joseph F Wehner	American	5	2	6
Hans Weiss	German	5	-	16

* William G Barker and Harold B Hudson of No 28 Sqn shared in the destruction of five Austro-Hungarian balloons over Fossmerlo on 12 February 1918

Artist Harry Dempsey has created the colour profiles for this volume, working closely with the Author so as to portray the aircraft as accurately as circumstances permit. Some of the illustrations are, admittedly, reconstructions based on fragmentary photographic evidence or descriptions provided by the pilots while they were alive, combined with known unit marking policy.

1

Nieuport 16 N880 of Sous-Lt Charles Nungesser, N65, Lemmes, May 1916

Not all of Charles Nungesser's aircraft bore his familiar black heart with white skull and crossbones. N880, in which he scored his early fighter victories, wore a simple initial on the fuselage sides and upper decking, as was commonly done for many of N65's pilots at the time. Nungesser probably flew this machine to burn a balloon on 2 April 1916, and to destroy one of six *Drachen* (out of eight intended targets) during the multiple-aeroplane operation of 22 May 1916.

2

SPAD XIII (serial unknown) of Sous-Lt Gilbert Sardier, SPA77, Fére-en-Tardenois, spring 1918

Exemplifying the colourful markings used by *'Les Sportifs'* of SPA77, Gilbert Sardier's early Blériot-built SPAD XIII sports what seems to be the number '8' in the same gold used for the *escadrille's* Cross of Jerusalem emblem with red highlighting, as well as a white cowl and camshaft covers, white tail and red elevators. A 'team player' among *'Les Sportifs'*, Sardier shared all five of his balloon victories (out of a total of 14) with other members of SPA77.

3

SPAD XIII (serial unknown) of Sous-Lt Maurice Jean-Paul Boyau, SPA77, Fére-en-Tardenois, spring 1918

Boyau's penchant for balloon-busting is reflected in the Le Prieur rocket tubes he had mounted on the inner set of interplane struts of his early Blériot-built SPAD XIII. Boyau was credited with 15 aeroplanes destroyed, and had just exploded his 20th *Drachen* when he was shot down in flames on 16 September 1918.

4

SPAD VII (serial unknown) of Sgt Pierre Cardon, SPA81, June 1918

The camouflage pattern of this SPAD VII, partially shown on one of Cardon's photographs, is provisional, although the markings are clear enough. Cardon shared in the destruction of five balloons, the last of which he flew through as it exploded on 6 June 1918.

5

Nieuport 16 N978 of Sgt Joseph Henri Guiguet, N95, Lemmes, May 1916

After conducting early tests of Yves Le Prieur's new anti-balloon rockets in N976 in April 1916, Guiguet used N978 when he joined seven other volunteers in the weapon's first operational use on 22 May 1916 – in his case, destroying the

Drachen at Sivry-sur-Meuse. It was Guiguet's sole balloon success, but a significant one. Later serving in N3 and SPA167, Guiguet finally reached acedom in October 1918.

6

SPAD VII (serial unknown) of Sous-Lt Claude Haegelen, SPA100, Champaubert, June 1918

This somewhat provisional SPAD VII is believed to have been used by Sous-Lt Claude Haegelen to score some of his early successes with SPA100. Already victor over two aircraft while with SPA103, he downed another 20 with SPA100 to become its leading ace. All but one of Haegelen's twelve balloon victories were collaborative efforts, including one shared with Sous-Lt Gilbert Sardier of SPA77 on 30 June 1918, and two with Sous-Lt Maurice Boyau of that neighbouring unit on 1 July and 14 September.

7

SPAD XIII (serial unknown) of Sous-Lt Léon Jean-Pierre Bourjade, SPA152, La Noblette, June 1918

This Blériot-built SPAD XIII continued Bourjade's practice, begun on a Nieuport, of affixing a pennant of the Sacré Coeur amid the French tricolour behind his cockpit. The scout also apparently had a partial white fuselage band and part of the headrest painted red, as well as a portrait of his patron, Sainte Thérèse, below and in front of the cockpit. Obsessed with revenge against the balloons that had directed artillery fire against him and his comrades when he was an infantryman, Bourjade destroyed 27 *Drachen* and one aeroplane before resuming his training for the priesthood post-war.

8

SPAD VII S3098 of Sgt Paul Armand Petit, SPA154, Villeneuve-des-Vertus, June 1918

After downing an Albatros on 3 April 1918, Parisian Paul Petit was probably flying this SPAD when he, Michel Coiffard and Louis Gros burned a balloon at Corroil on 30 June 1918. He went on to score four more victories – three of them balloons – before being killed while flying Blériot-built SPAD XIII S15060 on 18 September 1918, in the same action that also cost SPA154 its second-ranking ace, Jacques Ehrlich.

9

SPAD XIII (serial unknown) of Lt Michel Coiffard, SPA154, Trecon, August 1918

Commander and leading ace of SPA154, Lt Michel Coiffard flew an Adolphe Bernard-built SPAD XIII in the late summer of 1918 with red wheels, as well as the *escadrille's* red band and cowl – *MADO* referred to one of his girlfriends. SPA154 flew numerous anti-balloon missions, and most of their aces' scores – including Coiffard's – were shared team efforts.

10

SPAD XIII S7921 of Adjutant Jacques Ehrlich, SPA154, Trecon, September 1918

In September 1918, SPA154 replaced its red fuselage band with a crane within a light blue panel. Adolphe Bernard-built SPAD XIII S7921 probably had that new insignia when Ehrlich scored his final victories in it, taking his score to 18 balloons and one aeroplane before his luck ran out on 18 September 1918, when he was brought down and taken prisoner.

11

SPAD VII (serial unknown) of Sous-Lt Georges Lachmann, N581, Kamenets-Podolsk, autumn 1917

Lachmann flew this SPAD in Russia. In addition to the synchronised Vickers machine gun, he sometimes added both a Lewis gun on a makeshift overwing mounting and Le Prieur rockets for balloon-busting missions. Three of his five successes in Russia were over *Drachen*.

12

Hanriot HD 1 Nº 23 of Sous-Lt Willy Coppens, *9ème Escadrille Belge*, Les Moëres, September 1918

By mid-September, Sous-Lt Willy Coppens was flying Nº 23, which was equipped with an 11 mm gun and a Lanser self-sealing fuel tank. The fighter was painted royal blue like his earlier H 1 Nº 6 had been, as well as Nº 45, and was fitted with an enlarged HD 2 rudder. Assigned to the ace as a reserve machine, Nº 23 was used by Coppens on 14 October 1918 when he destroyed his last two *Drachen*, but paid for them with his left leg.

13

Camel F2153 of Lt George R Riley, No 3 Sqn, Valheureux, September 1918

London-born Lt George Riley scored the last three of his five balloon victories while flying Camel F2153 on 27 September 1918, burning the first two at 0805 hrs and sharing the third's destruction with 2Lt W H Maxted. The following day he downed a Fokker D VII for his 13th, and final, aerial success.

14

SE 5a B8422 of Capt Tom Falcon Hazell, No 24 Sqn, Bertangles, August 1918

Capt Hazell used SE 5a B8422 to down two Fokker D VIIs and a two-seater before burning two balloons – one of which was shared with 2Lt John A Southey – on 21 August. In the course of 'roasting a third sausage' on the 22nd, however, Hazell was badly shot-up and chased practically all the way home by a persistent Fokker D VII that left his aeroplane a write-off. Although Hazell survived to finish the war with 43 victories, of which ten were over balloons, he was credited that day to *Jasta* 4 commander, and second-ranking German ace, Oblt Ernst Udet as his 60th victory.

15

Camel B6313 of Capt William G Barker, No 28 Sqn, Grossa, spring 1918

Photographed on its back with a sheepish looking Barker smiling alongside after a rough landing, B6313 had had its original 'C1' marking replaced by the letter 'N' sometime after its arrival in Italy, and the scout would go through further marking changes as it followed Barker to Nos 66 and 139 Sqns. Barker scored all of his nine balloon victories with No 28 Sqn, including five in one sortie in concert with fellow Canadian Lt Harold B Hudson. Those successes pale alongside the 50 overall victories and the Victoria Cross that Barker amassed by the end of the war, however.

16

SE 5a D5984 of Lt William E Shields, No 41 Sqn, Conteville, August 1918

Although he was credited with shooting down six aircraft while flying D5984 between 28 June and 11 August 1918, William Shields scored all five of his balloon victories later in SE 5a C1912. Born in Lipton, Saskatchewan, on 15 October 1892, Shields survived the war with 24 victories, but was killed in a flying accident while serving in the Royal Canadian Air Force in 1920.

17

Camel B6402 of Capt Henry W Woollett, No 43 Sqn, Touquin, spring 1918

A medical student before the war, and a veteran of the ill-fated 1915 Dardanelles campaign, Henry Woollett had already become an ace flying de Haviland DH 2s and DH 5s with No 24 Sqn by the time he transferred to No 43 Sqn in March 1918. There, he gained fame on 12 April 1918 when he became the second British pilot to claim six victories in one day – the other, John L Trollope, being a squadronmate. An exhibitionist by RAF standards, Woollett wore a leopard-skin flying helmet and gauntlets, and decorated his spinner with a red Indian's face as well as a green dragon badge on the fuselage side of his Camel. He also briefly applied white patches to his scout as experimental camouflage for balloon sorties until his superiors advised him to remove them. Even without that, he destroyed two balloons on 27 March 1918, three more on 2 April, two on 22 April, one on 9 May, one on 15 July and two on 19 July. Woollett survived the war with 35 victories overall, and died on 31 October 1969.

18

Camel D6418 of Lt Donald R MacLaren, No 46 Sqn, Berck-sur-Mer, May 1918

Don MacLaren was commanding 'C' Flight, and already had three previous balloons and 21 aeroplanes to his credit, when he shared in the destruction of a DFW C V and burned two more *Drachen* south of Steenwerck on 20 May 1918 in Camel D6418. By the time a broken leg, suffered during a friendly wrestling match with a squadronmate on 10 October 1918, invalided him out of No 46 Sqn, MacLaren's total had reached 48 aeroplanes and six balloons destroyed.

19

SE 5a D6586 of Capt Anthony F W Beauchamp-Proctor, No 84 Sqn, Bertangles, August 1918

Tony Beauchamp-Proctor led No 84 Sqn's 'C' Flight in D6586 – hence the blue and white wheel hub – in which he also added 11 enemy aeroplanes and five balloons (including two on 22 August) to his tally between 8 August and 7 September 1918. His total came to 38 aeroplanes and 16 balloons destroyed, which, combined with his work as flight leader and ground strafer as the frontline situation required, earned him the Victoria Cross.

20

SE 5a E4071 of Lt Sidney W Highwood, No 84 Sqn, Assevillers, September 1918

Already victor over four aeroplanes and four balloons, Sidney Highwood used this red-wheeled 'A' Flight SE 5a to destroy three more balloons on 24 September 1918, followed by a further two on the 29th and two Fokker D VIIs on 3 October. A Fokker downed while flying E5073 on 30 October brought his total up to 16. E4071 was subsequently used by 'A' Flight's South African leader, Capt Walter A Southey, to down a balloon on 14 October and a Fokker D VII on the 27th (out of a total of five balloons and 15 aeroplanes credited to him).

21
Camel E1416 of Capt Arthur H Cobby, No 4 Sqn, AFC, Serny, September 1918

Capt Arthur Cobby's last Camel, E1416 figured in at least eight of his 29 victories, including his last of five balloons on 14 July 1918. The AFC's top-scorer, Cobby was also its only balloon ace. Aside from the standard drab post-22 March 1918 markings, the ace screwed an aluminium cut-out of Charlie Chaplin to each of the plywood fuselage sides below his cockpit! One survives at the RAAF Museum at Point Cook, in Victoria.

22
Nieuport 11 Ni 2265 of Sottotenente Giovanni Ancillotto, 77ª Squadriglia, Marcon, November 1917

The closest thing the Italians had to a balloon ace, Giovanni Ancillotto was credited with three, all while flying an 'expendable' Nieuport 11 armed with Le Prieur rockets. He gained particular renown on 5 December 1917 when he flew through his third *Drachen*. Ancillotto's overall score was 11.

23
SPAD XIII S15836 of 2Lt Frank Luke Jr, 27th Aero Squadron, Rembercourt, September 1918

After months of acquiring a sorry reputation as the 'Arizona Boaster', 2Lt Frank Luke burned a *Drachen* while flying this Blériot-built SPAD on 12 September 1918 – after which it was withdrawn to the 1st Air Depot at Colombey-les-Belles. This scout was the first of several aeroplanes that Luke would write off in the course of destroying 14 balloons and four enemy fighters over the next 17 days. His last, Adolphe Bernard-built SPAD S7984, had just been delivered to the 27th Aero Squadron and had not had any markings applied to it when, on 29 September 1918, Luke took it up for the sortie that brought him his last three successes, death and a posthumous Medal of Honor.

24
SPAD XIII S15169 of 1Lt Harvey Weir Cook, 94th Aero Squadron, Rembercourt, September 1918

Four of Harvey Weir Cook's seven victories were over balloons – a record within the 94th Aero Squadron second only to the five credited to his commander, Capt Eddie Rickenbacker. Awarded the DSC with oak leaf, Cook served in the US Army Air Forces in World War 2, but was killed in 1943 when his Curtiss P-40 crashed in New Zealand.

25
SPAD XIII S15123 of 1Lt Lansing C Holden Jr, 95th Aero Squadron, Touquin, July 1918

Seven days after transferring from French *escadrille* N471 to the 95th Aero Squadron on 20 July 1918, 'Denny' Holden described his SPAD XIII's markings thus, 'The numbers are white, red bordered, also the bands – three bands for the third flight (on the upper wing) – also a white nose. The mule is our squadron insignia'. Five of Holden's seven victories were over balloons.

26
LFG Roland D IIa (Pfal) 2876/16 of Ltn Hans Pippart, Jagdkommando, Flieger Abteilung 220, Galician Front, summer 1917

Fast and rugged, but heavy on the controls, the LFG Roland D II 'Haifisch' (shark) was an unpopular dogfighter but a suitable balloon hunter. Ltn Hans Pippart used this Pfalz-built 'Haifisch' in support of the German *Südarmee* in Galicia, downing two Russian aeroplanes and four balloons between 25 May and 23 October 1917. He would add two balloons and 14 aeroplanes to his account over the Western Front before being killed in action on 11 August 1918.

27
Albatros D III D.2243/16 of Ltn Heinrich Gontermann, Jasta 5, Boistrancourt, April 1917

During 'Bloody April' 1917, *Jasta* 5's *Albatrosen* used black numbers on the fuselage and on both undersides of the lower wing, midway between fuselage and crosses. Ltn Gontermann's aeroplane had a field-applied green stipple over earth brown, similar to a personal camouflage scheme he would later use in *Jasta* 15. Gontermann began his reign of terror against the Allied balloon line with one from the French 41e *Compagnie* on 8 April 1917, one from the 55e on the 13th, followed by two British gasbags on the 16th, two on the 22nd (only one of which was confirmed) and one from the 8th Kite Balloon Section, 1st Brigade, 1st Wing (8-1-1) on the 26th. His overall tally stood at 17 at the end of April, when he was given command of *Jasta* 15.

28
Fokker D VII (F) 5056/18 of Ltn Friedrich Noltenius, Jasta 6, Metz-Frescaty, October 1918

Born in Bremen on 8 January 1894, Friedrich Noltenius had a red band in the colours of his native city applied to his Fokker D VII of *Jasta* 27 – in which he scored 13 victories, including four balloons – and later on Fokker-built, BMW-engined, D VII (F) 5056/18 after his transfer to *Jasta* 6 on 27 September 1918. He used this machine to burn an American gasbag of the 10th Balloon Company at Bois de Puvenelle on 6 October, followed by a SPAD at Fontaine on the 10th, before a personality clash with his *Staffelführer*, Ltn Ulrich Neckel, led to his transfer to *Jasta* 11 on the 19th. Noltenius downed three more aeroplanes and three balloons with that famous unit, but the German collapse prevented him from receiving the *Orden Pour le Mérite*.

29
Fokker Dr I 450/18 of Ltn Josef Jacobs, Jasta 7, Ste Marguerite, October 1918

Preferring the nimble Fokker triplane over the D VII, Josef Jacobs kept at least two black Dr Is flying in spite of Germany's lack of suitable lubrication for their rotary engines by offering a case of champagne to any infantryman who recovered replacement engines from British aircraft downed in their lines. This Dr I's fuselage was originally decorated with an ornate fire-breathing devil's head, but may have been refinished black overall for the war's final weeks. Some 30 of Jacobs' 41 victories were scored in Dr Is – a record for the type – including six of his eight accredited balloons.

30

Albatros D III (OAW) (serial unknown) of Ltn Erich Löwenhardt, *Jasta* 10, Marcke, September 1917

Built by OAW (Ostdeutsch Albatros Werke), this Albatros D III featured the more rounded rudder of that firm's products, along with *Jasta* 10's yellow nose, '15' below the cabane struts and Löwenhardt's personal marking of a white wavy line on the fuselage sides and upper wing. Wings and tailplane were probably in green and mauve uppersurfaces, with light blue undersides. Löwenhardt's first victory was over a balloon of the French 58e *Compagnie* on 24 March 1917, and he would burn another French one on 9 September, followed by British gasbags on 21 September and 14 October. In 1918, he would add more to his tally on 5 January, 12, 15 and 21 March and on 20 May. The rest of his 54 victories were over aeroplanes, before the third-ranking German ace was killed in action on 10 August 1918.

31

Albatros D V (serial unknown) of Oblt Heinrich Gontermann, *Jasta* 15, Le Clos Ferme, Boncourt, autumn 1917

Although Germany's second-ranking balloon ace with 17, Heinrich Gontermann balanced such missions against the responsibilities of leadership and more conventional fighter sorties, scoring a total of 39 victories. His Albatros D V was overpainted in a silvery grey finish, with dark green dapple camouflage, which was somewhat contradicted by a red band and red, white and black leader's streamers affixed to the tailplane.

32

Albatros D III D.2033/16 of Vzfw Julius Buckler, *Jasta* 17, St Quentin-le-Petit, April 1917

This early Albatros D III had a centre-mounted radiator on the upper wing and its uppersurfaces painted in green and brown camouflage. At that time, *Jasta* 17's markings apparently consisted of fuselage bands with either white or black predominating, depending on the flight. Buckler used this aeroplane to score his first balloon victory – a gasbag of the French 36e *Compagnie* – over Boise de Génicourt at 0930 hrs on 26 April 1917. Later, flying two Albatros D Vs, named *Mops* and *Lilly*, he destroyed a British balloon at Neuville on 29 October and another at Laventie on the 31st. Commissioned a leutnant on 18 November, Buckler downed two balloons and an RE 8 on the same day, followed by another gasbag on the 29th. His last was claimed over Tricot on 3 May 1918 and Buckler was given command of *Jasta* 17 on 22 September. He survived the war with 35 confirmed victories, dying in Berlin on 23 May 1960, aged 66.

33

Albatros D Va (serial unknown) of Ltn Friedrich Röth, *Jasta* 16b, St Marguerite, May 1918

After a 'dry spell' of more than a month, 'Fritz' Röth resumed his balloon rampage with a vengeance on 29 May 1918, single-handedly destroying five balloons and forcing five others to be winched down. His Albatros D Va, which apparently had a black and white fuselage band as well as Bavarian *Jasta* 16's black tail *Staffelfarbe* and five-colour lozenge wing camouflage, returned from the mission thoroughly shot-up and virtually a write-off. Röth's score by 11 November 1918 stood at 20 balloons and eight aeroplanes (not bad for a pilot who claimed to have had poor eyesight), but depression over the war's outcome led him to commit suicide on New Year's Eve.

34

Pfalz D IIIa 8009/17 of Ltn Friedrich Höhn, *Jasta* 21s, St Mard, March 1918

This aeroplane featured the black and white fuselage band behind the cockpit of Saxon *Jasta* 21 and 'Fritz' Höhn's initials and red bands, which were designed to confuse enemy gunners – similar to those he had previously applied to his Pfalz D III. He also braced a Teddy bear mascot behind the cockpit. After downing a Breguet 14 on 1 December 1917, Höhn burned a French balloon of 36e *Compagnie* on 11 April 1918, another the following day, and a double success over gasbags of 45e and 21e *Compagnies* on 20 April. Later flying a Fokker D VII, he destroyed more balloons on 20 and 22 August, then served as acting commander of *Jasta* 81 before taking command of *Jasta* 60. With the latter unit, Höhn burned more French balloons on 15 and 26 September, and on the 28th he destroyed one from the French 67e *Compagnie* at Tahure and a second from the 6th US Balloon Company at Bethelainville. Höhn had been credited with 21 victories by the time he was mortally wounded in combat over St Martin l'Heureux on 3 October 1918.

35

Albatros D III D.607/17 of Ltn Heinrich Bongartz, *Jasta* 36, St Loup, May 1917

Ltn Heinrich Bongartz reportedly had the name *'Laura'* painted below the cockpit on the left side of his Albatros D III D.607/17, although photographic evidence of this has not turned up. His first victory, on 6 April 1917, was over a SPAD VII in which Lt Jean Mistarley of SPA31 had just burnt a balloon at Lavannes. Soon afterward, Bongartz went on a brief balloon spree of his own, destroying two French balloons on 27 April, another two on 20 May and his fifth – and last – three days later. Awarded the *Orden Pour le Mérite* on 23 December 1917, his total score came to 33 victories.

36

Fokker D VII (serial unknown) of Ltn Georg Meyer, *Jasta* 37, Neuville, September 1918

Born in Bremen on 11 January 1893, Georg Meyer had served in the infantry prior to flying two-seaters over Macedonia and the Western Front, where he scored his first victory with Fl. Abt. 253 on 7 February 1917. In April he joined *Jasta* 22, then accompanied Josef Jacobs on 2 August to *Jasta* 7, with which unit he destroyed a balloon on the 14th. Meyer had added two Camels to his score when he transferred to *Jasta* 37 on 25 March 1918, and became its commander on 14 April. He burned more balloons on 17 June and 13 and 17 July, and was flying this Fokker D VII when he destroyed two more on 10 and 14 October. Meyer survived the war with a total of 24 victories, but was killed in a motorcycle accident on 15 September 1926.

37
Fokker D VII (serial unknown) of Vzfw Oskar Hennrich, Jasta 46, Moislains, September 1918
Ltn Otto Creutzmann changed Jasta 46's marking from green and yellow tail chevrons to a black nose and white tail after taking command of the unit on 5 June 1918. Oskar Hennrich's personal initial may have been deep yellow as shown, or red or black. His Albatros-built D VII had a BMW engine and a replacement lower wing in four-colour lozenge camouflage from an OAW machine – all indicative of the punishment his fighter endured during the course of the many balloon hunting sorties that eventually brought him 13 gasbags destroyed, out of 20 victories overall.

38
Albatros D Va (serial unknown) of Ltn Martin Demisch, Jasta 58, Ennemain, June 1918
Born in Bautzen on 12 November 1896, Martin Demisch (also spelt Dehmisch in some sources) began his scoring with Jasta 58 by burning a balloon on 16 June 1918, and two on the 18th. Later flying Fokker D VIIs, he added three more aircraft to his tally, as well as more balloons on 6 and 13 September, but after downing an SE 5a of No 40 Sqn on 24 September, he was brought down near Abancourt by other members of that unit and died of his injuries the next day.

39
Albatros D Va (serial unknown) of Ltn Max Näther, Jasta 62, Balâtre, June 1918
Max Näther's Albatros D Va, and later Fokker D VII, bore the black fuselage with red nose of Jasta 62, with the Imperial German flag as a personal marking. After downing a SPAD XIII on 16 May, he scored a quick succession of victories over French balloons on 1, 5, 7, 16, 27 and 28 June. Still 18 when he was given command of his Staffel on 7 July, Näther ultimately raised his tally to 26, including another French and three American balloons, but the war ended before his recommendation for the Orden Pour le Mérite could be approved.

40
Albatros D III (Oef) 153.209 of Oblt Godwin Brumowski, Fliegerkompagnie 41J, Portobuffole, June 1918
Inspired by Manfred von Richthofen's livery while visiting the Western Front in the early months of 1917, Godwin Brumowski painted at least two of his Oeffag-built Albatros D IIIs red overall, with the addition of his skull personal marking. His final aeroplane, 153.209 was used to destroy the last of the five balloons credited to him. Brumowski claimed his first over Spresiano on 16 June, and on the 19th he downed a second near Passarella, subsequently sharing in bringing down an Italian two-seater south of Candelu and then downing an Ansaldo SVA 5 over Montello for his 35th, and final, wartime victory.

BIBLIOGRAPHY

Willy Coppens de Houthulst, Days on the Wing, Arno Press, New York, NY, 1980
Norman L R Franks, letter in Over the Front, Vol 17, No 1, Spring 2002. pp.89-90
Norman L R Franks, Frank W Bailey and Russell Guest, Above the Lines, Grub Street, London, 1993
Norman L R Franks, Russell Guest and Gregory Alegi, Above the War Fronts, Grub Street, London, 1997
Norman L R Franks and Frank W Bailey, Over the Front, Grub Street, London, 1992
Norman L R Franks and Frank W Bailey, The Storks, Grub Street, London, 1998
Roberto Gentilli, Antonio Iozzi and Paolo Varriale, Italian Aces of World War 1 and their Aircraft, Schiffer Publishing Ltd, Atglen, Pa, 2003
Jon Guttman, 'Triumphs and Tribulations: Pierre de Cazenove de Pradines', Cross & Cockade (USA) Journal, Vol 21, No 1, Spring 1980
David Hide, 'Half a Pair of Wings', Cross & Cockade International Journal, Vol 27, No 3, Autumn 1996, pp118-140
Francis Lombardi, 'Gli Amici di Marcon – 1918-1978', Cross & Cockade (Great Britain) Journal, Vol 12, No 3, Fall 1981, pp 118-129
Walter A Musciano, 'The Eagle of the Aegean Sea', Aviation History, September 1999
Donald R Neate, '"Proccy" to his Friends', Cross & Cockade (Great Britain) Journal, Vol 8, No 1, Spring 1977, pp 25-32
Thomas Nilsson, 'Jean-Pierre Bourjade, The Pilot of St Thérèse', Over the Front, Vol 1, No 2, Summer 1988

'War Diary of Friedrich Noltenius', Cross & Cockade (USA) Journal, Vol 7, No 4, Winter 1966, pp 329-342
Dr Martin O'Connor, Air Aces of the Austro-Hungarian Empire 1914-1918, Champlin Fighter Museum Press, Mesa, Ariz, 1986
Neal W O'Connor, 'Hans Pippart – An Ace From Baden', Over the Front, Vol 1, No 1, Spring 1986, pp 25-31
Daniel Porret, Les 'As' français de la Grande Guerre, Service Historique de l'Armée de l'Air, Château de Vincennes, 1983
Eddie V Rickenbacker, Fighting the Flying Circus, Avon Books, New York, NY, 1965
Peter Schiemer, Die Albatros (Oeffag) Jagdflugzeuge der k.u.k. Luftfahrturppen, Herbert Weishaupt Verlag, Graz, Austria, 1984
Alan D Toelle, 'Frank Luke's Spad #21', Over the Front, Vol 19, No 2, Summer 2004, pp 118-121
Gregory J W Urwin, 'The Blue Devil of Belgium', Air Classics, January 1981
Greg VanWyngarden, 'Richthofen's Circus', Jagdgeschwader Nr 1, Osprey Publishing, Oxford, England, 2004, pp 111-113
George H Williams, 'Louis Bennett Jr, No 40 Sqn, RFC, RAF', Cross & Cockade (USA) Journal, Vol 21, No 4, Winter 1980, pp 331-350
George H Williams, 'Louis Bennet Jr, No 40 Sqn, RFC, RAF, A Postscript', Cross & Cockade (USA) Journal, Vol 25, No 3, Autumn 1984, pp 242-245
La Vie Aérienne Illustrée, 1917-18

INDEX

References to illustrations are shown in **bold**. Plates are shown with page and caption locators in brackets.